Moneycall

A Proactive Sales Method for <u>Recurring Sales</u>

with less prospecting

BY

ERIKUNLE JOHN

MONEY Call

A Proactive Sales Method for Recurring Sales with less prospecting

Erikunle John

Table of Contents

INTRODUCTION

In December 2022 I saw Billy Beane, the Oakland A's executive at a HARDI conference, and it surprised me how much his approach to baseball had a similar spin to what we were implementing with several organizations on the sales front. The book that showcased Beane "Moneyball" was a sensation as it explained how a data and analysis way of looking at baseball would help smaller teams that could not compete in the same level as larger more powerful teams. Our data analysis happened to provide a different result and that was: *Recurring sales businesses should concentrate in nurturing, understanding and growing from their current customers and not in prospecting so much.* That may go against a lot of sales training "gurus" yet data does not lie. Many distributors in the HVACR industry (a recurring sale industry) drive more than 80% of their sales from less than 20% of their customers on their database. As more and more companies concentrated in being proactive by calling their "forgotten" customers systematically, their sales soared. From that "AHA" moment came the idea to name the book "MoneySales" since you will see how much data and systems have more to do with B2B sales success than applying "new and improved" sales techniques. Later on, when we realized the effectiveness of measuring different types of calls, we decided that the book title should be "Moneycall", a PROACTIVE system to generate more sales and to control its process.

The other side of Billy's approach was the fact that he questioned certain assumptions about the way the game operated. You will see that we challenge several ideas about selling, especially in "recurring and frequent sales" that has made many "professional sales trainers" doubt that one could be successful in sales without PROSPECTING. When you are proactive, many ideas about sales go out the door. The key is to use your data to serve more than to sell. The numbers will provide a clear guideline for many different ideas, and the story in the novel will provide a "live in the trenches" way to see the analysis based on real situations and comparable data from various organizations.

The mission of the book is to put you in a context where you need to change a successful organization and make it better, without hiring "stars" for your sales team. All you need to do is hire people that are willing to follow a system to generate more sales, serve their clients better and help everybody make more money; Capitalism at its best.

Another key to understanding the system is the fact that salespeople have a finite bandwidth, and that it is determined by the number of accounts and calls that they can handle. Plus, there is a difference between the types of calls and the way to measure those calls. The basic premise is: If you manage the activities that produce results, the results will show up automatically. This is a very liberating reality for sales managers, as you do not need to wait for the end of the month to predict what the outcome of a particular salesperson will be.

Please do not let the simplicity of the system or the story fool you, the key is in the implementation. The reason we made it a novel is to show each step, based on how the implementation has been done in other organizations, so you can copy those same steps and start producing results quickly in your own company. At the end of the story we want to show that viable ideas are still going to come that will improve the current Moneycall system. Perhaps you, yes you the Reader, are the person to come up with that idea. If so, please look us up on LinkedIn and drop us a line to set up a call to keep improving the system. The important thing is that with simple tools (one included in this book) and with the software and phone systems available today any organization can implement Moneycall and be very successful.

ACKNOWLEDGMENTS

I have been very fortunate to have been part of a great industry and I am continually thriving with the help of so many wonderful individuals. On the other hand, I certainly could not have written this book without getting several organizations involved, which needed to take control of their sales process instead of waiting for clients to buy from them. The principles included in the Moneycall system, came from observation, analysis and frustrations from the processes that didn't work. The proactivity of the system provides the control and "predictability" that many business owners and salespeople are looking for. These experiences, support and opportunities must be acknowledged.

I first saw a proactive sales system at work at Autonation in Ft Myers Florida, where I was fortunate to take their training and in 3 months became the number one salesperson in the store, working at the internet sales department. I learned many great tools, KPIs and standards. Most importantly I had a lab to observe others perform the same tasks that I was doing. I could look at their results vs mine. By using my Industrial Engineering background - which I never expected to use in sales, I noticed how the system operated and took many engineering ideas to implement a better and more logical sales process. After I recognized that HVACR Distribution was a "recurring sales industry" many new ideas started to click. One of the first things I applied in our industry was not to look for new leads and to concentrate on "nurturing" our customers by following up and emailing. This was the first sign that being proactive paid dividends vs those that never followed up. I later moved to the east coast of Florida leaving Ft Myers behind, yet the lessons learned there were invaluable.

I also must thank Ed Morse in Delray beach for the opportunity to work in their internet department and to learn a new system that also gave me more ideas which allowed me to become the number one salesperson in their internet sales department. I was never a great salesman, but I was a great system follower and armed with perseverance and determination I quickly learned that a system is more important than salesmanship.

It is vital that I mention the management consulting firm that later became part of RSM, The

Vila del Corral Company. This talented group literally pushed me to start a career in sales with the line "before you implement any consulting you have to sell it". As a manager of the office, I did not have a choice, even if I disliked sales (and I did, remember I was an IE working on an MBA and sales was "beneath me"). I never expected sales to be in my future, and looking back at the growth that sales has given me both professionally and mentally, I now feel that it was the best thing that ever happened to me.

And although it is too many to name, I would be remiss if I did not thank all the sales people, corporations, friends, teachers, authors and consultants who have showered me with their wisdom. I mention some in the story of the book and I decided that I had to create a special section of the book for these "influencers". These are the giants that allowed me to stand on their shoulders and have shaped my thinking. It's a special section for me and I hope it also provides guidance for you.

I have had a lot of help implementing the concepts taught in this book. The members from HARDI whom I feel so blessed to have in my life are all greatly responsible for the achievements that made this journey possible. More importantly, those who have taken the time to discuss with us how they work and why the system that we propose made sense to them even if they have not yet started to implement it. To the different companies that have shown us their operation and their desire to improve and selflessly shared their best practices with the division from Latin America. To all of you, thank you, without you this book could not materialize as it is truly a work of collaboration and inspiration.

DEDICATION

To Giangabriel my son,

I had a dream to have a son, and God made that dream come true, I thank Him for Giangabriel and continue to ask for wisdom so I can guide him in the best way possible and yet let him make his own trail which will certainly be very different than mine. To you as a token of our efforts to make a trail that society values, I dedicate this book.

To Victor Mora,

For putting me on the path that I am now, thanks to Vitico for this is the happiest path that any man can have in life, I owe that to you.

To my family,

For remaining positive and loving when I had to leave home looking for a new opportunity. The support from my sister Saly was invaluable in the new path that I have followed to be here today. I dedicate this book to all of them and especially to Saly

To my LATAM members from HARDI,

A very special dedication on a personal level to all of you, for allowing me to come into your lives and your businesses. My conversations with your leaders, spending time with your employees and managers, made me feel that I was part of a family and never a stranger in a foreign country. To all of you I also dedicate this book, it is your stories that make this book a real story.

To my Chérie,

Some people say that one of the most important decisions a man can make is to choose the right life partner. Some wise gurus say that to be totally happy we must be grateful. I have the best combination, blessed and grateful in all aspects of my life. Chérie, you are an important part of my new and wonderful path of abundance.

Special thanks to:

Andy Armstrong: Who has contributed enormously with the way the story is written and specifically with the recommendation for chapter 10 on a simplified version of the Maximum Sales Formula. I feel that the chapter added a more realistic way to implement the system quicker and reduces the need to think that 100% of the KPIs must be measured to start a Moneycall Department implementation. Andy, thanks so much for all your input.

Who should read this book and why?

There are 3 key reasons to read this book:

1. If you are in the distribution business or any other recurring sales business, your company has invested in attending sessions about "The threat of Amazon". The presentations covered many interesting topics, yet they all failed to mention one very important fact: Amazon depends on customers buying from them, and their model makes it very difficult for them to be

proactive. It would be extremely hard for Amazon to change into a phone driven strategy and even more on an outbound, proactive basis to recurring customers. If your company is waiting for clients to call vs calling them proactively, then this book may help you create a competitive advantage.

2. If you live in a country where Amazon is not a threat yet or any other online competitor for that matter, are you sure that your regular competition is not going to change their strategy from a reactive to a proactive selling model? If you don't want to wait to find out, this book will help you get new ideas to have an advantage over your current competition.

3. If your business has had great sales results in the last few years, and you see those results are slowing down. If your phone rings less

than it used to, then this book will show you how to be more in control of your sales by contacting and learning more about your current customers.

If any of these reasons sound logical to you, then please read on.

CHAPTER 1

IT ALL STARTED WITH A CHALLENGE.

"Hey Leo, finally wrapping up the grand tour?" his co-worker, Mark, asked with a smile as he approached him.

Leo: Yeah, it's been quite a journey. I started right here, lifting boxes, and now I've seen every part of this business.

Mark: I remember you on your first day, all enthusiastic and eager to learn. You've come a long way. *Mark remarked, clapping him on the shoulder.*

Leo: Chuckled, "I had to start from the ground up, learn every part of the business. It's not just a job, it's our family's legacy."

Mark: Nodded, understandingly. "And you're doing a great job. It's not easy balancing the demands of this kind of work with the responsibilities of family expectations."

Leo: "Thanks Mark. It's challenging, but I believe in what we do here. And I've learned so much from everyone, including you.

As they walked back towards the office, Leo's thoughts were a mix of past hardships and future aspirations, firmly grounded in the values of hard work and dedication he had learned on the warehouse floor.

Leo was extremely happy after he completed his tour through the many departments of his family wholesale business. Three years ago, he had started in the warehouse, picking up boxes and doing the hard work that everyday millions of blue-collar workers do in distribution. Leo is brilliant, very observant and patient, an Industrial Engineer, he worked implementing JIT and other Japanese manufacturing techniques in an electronics and shoe manufacturing plants. He later got his MBA with a specialty in marketing, when he started his professional life, he knew for sure, that he never wanted to be in sales. He felt that to be pushy and to bother people constantly was not what he was cut out to be. He would later find that he started with the wrong definition of what sales truly was. Like many engineers, he saw sales with the wrong set of glasses, it took time, observation, and the right influencers for that definition to change.

It was interesting that his last position, during his three-year companywide tour at LATAM Supply, was precisely in the sales department. He felt quite comfortable because the customers were always looking for him and he never had to be forceful at all. Analysis was a superpower for Leo, things needed to make sense and questioning the status quo was very commonplace for him. One of the things that kept running around in his mind was "why do I feel so comfy in this sales job?" That question opened his mind to thinking" who starts the sales process in our company, is it the customer or is it the salespeople? Do we really sell, or do customers come and buy? If they buy, then are we in control of the process or are we just dependent on their decision?"

From those questions, he understood that if the company became more proactive to start the sales process with a desire to serve better, most likely the results would surpass the great reality of today.

After his three years of wholesale distribution experience plus his manufacturing and process change experience, Leo felt he had a good idea of how the company worked. The previous questions had given him some insights into certain changes that could be made which most likely would produce better results for the company. So, he decided to have a conversation with his father, Tony the company CEO, to see if he would let him make some adjustments to the way the business operated, especially in the sales department.

Tony was finalizing the last touches on a new location that they wanted to open when Leo approached him with several ideas that could make the business more profitable. After a long discussion ranging from "how much would this cost?" to "that would never work!" Tony decided that perhaps the best way to really see what his son could do was to let him run the whole operation of the new location.

Leo was in total disbelief when Tony said: "we can argue all day long about what could be good or not and I certainly don't want to be just like my father, who never allowed me to implement anything new until he retired. So, let's see if you put your money where your mouth is. Would you manage the new location for one year and then we can compare the top performance KPIs of your operation vs our other 17 locations? "After a ten second pause in absolute silence, Tony continued: "Then, if you do better, we can implement the changes in the other locations. Now, if you are unsuccessful then we will continue to do things the same way as today. Do we have a deal? This is a yes or no question, right now?"

After Leo thought about it for a few seconds, he replied: "yes, I will do it" and he proceeded to leave the room, feeling enormous pressure on his shoulders, not certain what was the first thing that he needed to do.

On his drive home, Leo remembered his professor and consultant at his MBA course, Guy Galeti, who was very instrumental in shaping some of the ideas that Leo now had. So, he called Guy while he was driving. After the normal pleasantries, Leo explained the reason for his call and his newly accepted challenge. Guy listened attentively to what Leo was describing and then, said: "Leo, I understand you want to make some improvements and that means you will need to change some processes, but you can't change everything from the beginning, and you can't make changes everywhere in the company, so where do you think you need to start first?"

Leo always liked Guy since he was truly a great coach and almost never provided answers, he just asked great questions. After thinking about what

Guy just asked, Leo answered: "I need to begin by transforming the sales system. If we are going to beat the other locations, I need to generate more income per employee than the rest and I need to do it faster than the regular ramp up".

Guy asked, "How will you do that?"

"I truly don't know," Leo admitted, his tone contemplative. "But I feel that we really don't sell anything. Customers just call us, and we provide them with the product they request."

"Now, do you have data to back this assumption, Leo?" Guy asked.

"I don't need any data. I was there every day, and all I had to do was wait for the phone to ring, help the customer buy, and we closed a good percentage of the calls like that. It's a bit different for the territory managers who visit 25-30 clients per month, but for the inside sales or phone salespeople, it was just a matter of waiting for the season to start and BOOM, the phones were ringing off the hook."

"Ok, so the basic premise is that your customers bought from you, you did not sell anything. Meaning you were all reactive vs proactive, and you want to change that, correct?" Guy summarized.

"Right, yet now I am thinking about how I can get data to show that this is the case," Leo responded, a hint of determination in his voice.

Guy inquired, "Does your phone system track calls?"

"Absolutely. All I have to do is see what ratio of calls are incoming vs what number of calls are made by the salespeople. I will call Victor, my IT manager, and I am sure he will have the answer," Leo said.

"How come your current people do not make calls now and just wait for calls to come in?" Guy probed further.

Leo sighed. "I started to think about that. We measure everything from an incoming point of view: how long it takes to pick up the phone, hold time... I just think we never thought about doing things differently. We have so many calls coming in that perhaps we felt it was not necessary to do anything else. I also find that many salespeople think that quoting is selling. They provide a piece of paper with a price, they've done their job, and the customer will call back if they want it. That shows there is a training issue and a quality of interaction issue. We need to design a better system for our salespeople to be more successful."

"So maybe you don't need to call anybody. Now, if you did, do you think that the personality and training of the person handling incoming calls would be the same as a person who starts the call process?" Guy asked

"Guy, we are Industrial Engineers, and we believe in specialization, so we know it takes different training and perhaps different personalities," Leo explained. "Yet the key is: you can't do two things at the same time well."

"What do you mean, Leo?" Guy inquired, curious.

Leo elaborated, "I know the counter guys make calls sometimes, but they don't do them well because if a customer comes in while they are talking, what are they going to tell them? Should he say 'Hey, wait until I handle this call'? No way. That person drove here and needs to be served. So, I am certain that we need a special person for this new proactive role."

Guy nodded, then asked, "What about the people in your inside sales phone department, why can't they make those calls?"

"I was in that position, and the phone rings too frequently for me to think right," Leo explained. "And when I do decide to make a call, I never get into a rhythm where I can follow a specific customer and provide personalized service. Do you understand what I mean?"

Guy responded, "Not really, could you tell me more?"

Leo went further, "The inside salesperson doesn't have a set of customers to call; they have all of the company's customers available. Now, when you get 10 to 50 calls a day and your database has 1500 clients, the math is stacked against you being able to call the same customer every month and follow up on their purchases in a personalized way. It's just too random, and in recurring sales, the relationship you build is crucial. We need to understand what our customers really want. We're not a supermarket with thousands of customers; in our business, a handful of customers represent a large percentage of our volume. We need to change the process to fit that reality. It's pure Industrial Engineering; it's about making the process fit the type of industry we are in. Does it make more sense now?"

"Yes, it does," his mentor replied. "So, it's clear you need a new structure and different training for the new salespeople. How soon do you need to get the personnel and everything up and running?"

"I have about 30 days," Leo answered. "But now that you've got me focused on just changing the sales system, I'll ask some of the managers to implement the same processes we have in other departments. I'll also request some veterans due for a promotion to get things rolling."

"That sounds like a big challenge," Guy acknowledged. "Go ahead and start moving, and if you feel that I can help, please just give me a call."

They exchanged pleasantries, hung up, and continued with their day. For Leo, it was a significant step, as he now had a clearer focus on what his tasks needed to be to start on the right path.

CHAPTER 2

THE BIG MEETING

Leo spoke to his father and the HR manager, and they agreed on which supervisors could be promoted from the 17 locations to get things moving quickly. Tony had already thought about this move before, so it was well underway by the time Leo requested the personnel. Tony's big surprise was that Leo was going to manage sales himself from the start and it was a bit of a shock for him since his son had always been quite negative about sales.

Tony: "I am surprised you are going to take on this role, I admire that you are doing that, yet I question if starting at your weakest position is a smart decision?"

Leo: "I learned I had the wrong point of view when it came to sales, plus I also learned that if I am going to make a big difference in the company in a short amount of time, I need to be more efficient in the number of sales I produce with the amount of people we have. In the end, it is not so much about understanding sales, it is more about understanding a process and numbers. Those are things I do rather well, and I know you agree on that."

Tony laughed and turned with a grin on his face, "Ok, it is your party, so you do as you think you need to, I hope you are not getting too far ahead into trouble. Anyway, do as you see fit, and I am here if you need me."

Many would kill to have a father like that, and many would never want to be put in this situation, Leo was willing to tackle the challenge head on.

With three weeks to go, Leo rounded up the management team and they laid out a plan for each department. Soon after, they were set and doing their tasks and training their people. Every department had a clear plan, except the new Proactive Sales Department, Leo needed to come up with the new system in that short period of time to help get more products moving out the door. So basically, Leo knew this new system had to be an improvement on the Sales per employee KPI. Then, he had to train his salesperson, implement the metrics, and get results in three weeks. The good thing is that he was starting small in this department, and he kept the same structures in the counter department and the inside sales department. He still needed to make a big difference with his new proactive method to justify the extra headcount.

Victor came to Leo's office with the phone data requested, and quickly Leo realized that 93% of the calls on average were incoming and during peak season they could be as high as 99%, so only 7% to 1% of the calls were being made by the salespeople. His hunch was correct; the issue was how could he turn things around from there.

He needed to start training his people quickly and decided that he would continue to use the same selling methods that the other locations used: Counter sales for the customers coming into the store, Territory Managers for large accounts and Internet sales for customers that preferred to place orders online or to repeat orders frequently with one click.

Now the only big change was going to be in the new phone sales department for "outbound calls". What Leo did not understand who this salesperson was supposed to call? After many hours of frustration, he called Guy again.

"Hi Guy, how are you?"

Guy, noticing Leo's demeanor, responded, "I am super well, Leo. You sound excited and worried at the same time, what's going on?"

Leo, eager to share, explained, "I have data that shows our company is doing well in sales by being reactive to our clients. The report from Victor shows that over 90% of our calls are incoming, so it's clear that our clients are buying from us, we're not selling to them."

Guy recalled a relevant quote, "Wasn't it Gitomer who said that people don't like to be sold to but love to buy?"

"Yes," Leo agreed, "but I also know that being there to help people proactively leads to more business."

Guy, intrigued, asked, "That's a bold statement, Leo. Do you have data to back that up?"

Leo admitted, "I don't, and that's part of why I called. I'm convinced we need to initiate the process more often and control the selling process, but I'm unsure WHO we need to call."

Guy was curious, "What do you mean by 'being in control of the selling process'?"

Leo explained, "When we're reactive, we respond to customer requests without time to review their last order or what they haven't bought but might need. If we prepare before calling a customer and research their previous orders, we can ask questions to understand their problems. This proactive approach helps us serve our customers better without really 'selling'."

Guy answered, "So, you're talking about being proactive, like taking an offensive rather than a defensive position, using a sports analogy."

"Exactly," Leo agreed. "The issue is WHO to call. I can't make random calls or have one person handle our entire client database."

Guy suggested, "Is there a way to get data pointing you to the right customers to call?"

Leo thought aloud, "Maybe I just need to talk to our best customers in the new location."

"Why your best customers?" Guy inquired.

Leo explained, "They already like and buy from us. Now that we're moving closer, they'll likely appreciate us even more."

Guy summarized, "So, you're essentially looking to provide better service to your best customers."

Leo pondered Guy's summary, "Yes, that's it. Now I'm wondering if focusing on our best customers is truly the biggest opportunity we have.

Guy continued, "Leo, you need to use data in order to be able to get a better idea, making changes based on hunches is extremely outdated". They both laughed, and Guy asked: "Have you analyzed your number of customers, how many times they buy, how many are handled by the salespeople, etc?

"You are right, I am going to sit down with Victor and get some information to see what is really going on today in all locations, so we can come up with a better plan." Leo said.

Guy: "Great, that sounds like the perfect place to start."

Leo immediately met with Victor in front of a computer and started to get some data on the number of clients per store, how many had purchased in the last 12 to 24 months, how many customers did a typical counter person attend in a year and how many customers did the internal phone salespeople attend. The results were eye opening.

Each store had about 1500 clients in the database, yet only between 150-200 purchased regularly and each counter salesperson had between 150 to 300 clients in one year, yet 30 to 40 made most of the volume. Then, Leo decided to use a Pareto analysis to see those who were the 20% of customers that represented 80% of the sales. He was surprised to see that the number was relatively small, and it matched the 30-40 that made the most volume per each counter salesperson. The same was true for the phone inside sales department. It was the same clients that kept on calling to place orders. That did not match the number of customers that requested quotes and never bought. They had many more incoming calls for quotes that kept them busy yet those were clients who never bought. Leo noticed that a lot of the time spent on these incoming calls was "wasted". When you quote a customer fifteen times and they do not buy, they are just price shopping and will always prefer their current provider to you. If you had a lower price, they would use your price to get it from their current provider.

With all this data, Leo felt that he had a better idea about how to structure the new system as he decided to call Guy one more time.

Leo: "Guy, you will not believe what I just found."

Guy kept silent and just said, "Oh".

Leo continued: "The data pointed me in the right direction, a very small percentage of our clients represent a very large amount of our sales, yet the other guys we don't call, could be a gold mine."

Guy now said one of those guru-like lines that he was so famous for: "Your best customers want to be your customers. There is something you do for them that they like. Your marginal customers, they don't want to be your customers, they prefer for some reason, to buy more from your competitors."

Leo: "You surely hit the nail on the head, I just need to keep treating my best customers super well in our area and start understanding and caring for those customers who prefer to do more business elsewhere to see if I can increase the amount of business from them here. I feel that my proactive approach will help me to achieve that."

Guy: "Sounds to me like you got your answer on the WHO to call question". They both laughed again.

Leo: "Certainly, now I need to figure out how many clients I need to assign to this new salesperson and what kind of a system we will create to avoid being "salesy" and yet effective. I just want to help people buy, to serve vs to sell."

Guy: "Great, now should you not do some PROSPECTING as well? All new businesses should look for new prospects to get a higher number of clients.

Leo: "That is exactly what the data is telling me not to do, you see I already have a lot of customers who know us, have credit, they have a relationship with us of some kind, and we have not understood them well enough to make them bigger clients. I think that a lot of sales trainers come from industries where you need to find new clients frequently, like cars, real estate, or insurance sales. Now when it is B2B recurring sales, like our business of HVACR parts and equipment, I don't need to look for new clients as much, just get more business from the clients that for some reason don't buy primarily from me. I can certainly prospect once I get a handle on the 1300 or more clients that we barely touch in the new location area."

Guy: "That is a very interesting conclusion Leo, I think you are right, I never thought of it that way. Come to think of it, I have several B2B clients that are in a similar situation where they are 100% reactive, and I always felt that they spent too much time and resources prospecting. I am going to look at their data as well and see if the same situation applies.

Leo: "That would be great Guy, meanwhile I will get ready to serve my current clients better."

Guy: "That sounds like a great idea, remember people don't like to be sold. Now if you are going to start calling them, should you at least understand what is it that they buy?"

Leo: "We know what they buy, it's in our database, we are not calling any new clients, remember!".

Guy: "You are not getting my point, nobody buys products, they buy a solution to a problem, they have a reason why they buy from you or from the competition, it would be important to know what in particular they buy from the start."

Leo: "Wow Guy!You are right, so how do I get that information?"

Guy, laughed and then said: "you ask...it's simple, but you need to make sure that it is done in a way that the customer feels he is going to gain something from the information."

Leo: "Like always, I think you are on to something, let me think about what questions I need to incorporate into the system so my people can ask them".

Guy: "Sounds like a plan, let's stay in touch, I will see if the same numbers apply to my other B2B clients with recurring sales.

Leo: "Talk to you soon".

CHAPTER 3

THE 5 KEYQUESTIONS

Leo decided that he was going to talk to Estelle the corporate marketing manager to get some insights into what questions would provide the most feedback into WHAT clients buy. He explained to her the whole conversation with Guy, and that he needed to come up with a list of easy questions that could show the salesperson what the customer really bought.

Estelle: "I understand what you want Leo, I think you need to go straight to the point and ask directly, yet the key will be in the way the person listens to the answers, more than the question itself."

Leo: "What do you mean?"

Estelle: "Well, every time you do market research, itis imperative to let the customer provide information, not to be defensive or to sell anything, you must be smart to get information."

Leo: "That goes hand in hand with my definition of selling."

Estelle: "And what would that definition be Leo"? she asked with a grin on her face.

Leo: "Selling is getting information, not providing information. It means understanding what are the problems, the customer wants to solve, not to pitch products or ideas. So, if the salesperson is providing information, then he is not learning what the customer wants. When you tell... you don't learn.To learn... you must listen to determine the customer's problems."

Estelle: "That sounds more like marketing than selling. I must agree that if you do that, you will certainly sell more, and your sales process will be easier."

Leo: "Ok. What questions should the salesperson ask?"

Estelle: "Well, I want to know what it is that he likes about buying with us. Going from my research experience, his first answer will not be the most valuable, we will need to keep digging, while being attentive and listening."

Leo: "Great, I love that, what else?"

Estelle: "If the salesperson has dealt with the customer before they should ask: what do you like about doing business with me? Again, you will get things like: "You always call me back", but the key is to say, that is nice, I am glad that you like that, besides calling back, what else do you like about doing business with me? And you keep that trend until the customer says, "Well I guess that is it". Until you get that response, the salesperson needs to keep digging for information. This applies to all the questions."

Leo: "Sounds easy enough and logical, now what other questions should they ask?"

Estelle stayed quiet for a while and after 2 minutes looking at the ceiling she responded: "What do you like about doing business with the competition. Here, you don't need the competitors' name, you just need to understand what they like and value about doing business elsewhere, if they say a company name, its gravy, but the key is the information not the name. Come to think of it, it may be even better when they don't say a name because if they buy from more than 2 or 3 competitors, and our data shows they do, we will get feedback from what they value from all of them not just the name of the companies provided."

Leo: "Beautiful, now should you not also know what percentage of their total purchase comes from us?

Estelle: "Wow, that is a great question! It would allow us to know how much opportunity we have for growth and will keep the salesperson from thinking that he needs to call new clients, that alone would make my job in marketing a lot easier."

They both had a good laugh with that one.

Leo: "I surely get your point there. Our goal is not to do prospecting, at least at the beginning, but to understand and provide better service to our existing customers."

Estelle: "Yet, I feel that we are missing something. It is important for the customer to realize that we want to help him grow and not just to sell him something today. Perhaps that would be my challenge in marketing to convey that message."

Leo: "I understand Estelle, although the best way to make a customer, or any person for that matter, think about an issue, is to engage them with a question. Our goal here would be to ask in which particular market they are trying to grow and haven't been able to penetrate yet. Something like: What market has been particularly challenging for you to enter and how could we help you get customers in that niche?"

Estelle: "Uhm I love that one, it makes the customer think that we are here to serve and to help. At the same time, it positions us to be able to pull resources to assist them achieve their goals. After all, as a wholesaler, we have sold equipment and parts in every segment of the market in our state. So, I think that would be a great last question, Leo."

Leo: "Obviously the only change to the 5 Key Questions that we already planned, would be in case the salesperson never dealt with a specific customer. In that instance, it would not make sense to enquire what they liked about doing business with the salesperson."

Estelle: "I like that question because it provides positive reinforcement to the salesperson that the customer likes them, yet you are right we need an alternative".

Leo: "How about just knowing what has been particularly frustrating for them to find lately? Our goal here is to see if we can help them with that product."

Estelle: "Perfect, marketing 101 there! Let them tell you what they need, there is no better way to sell. I think you have your list, Leo."

Leo: "Thanks Estelle, let me start putting the system together so I can train my new telephone salesperson. I feel I should call this new proactive calls department, the Moneycall team, what do you think?"

That its certainly a catchy name, responded Estelle. I like it, so good luck hiring your Moneycall salesperson."

Leo departed, running merrily with his new idea taking shape in his head.

CHAPTER 4

TRAINING THE NEW PROACTIVE SALESPERSON

After a tough interview session with three candidates and using an index assessment test to select the final candidate, Leo sets the dates for his new salesperson, Laura, to start training on how to use the 5 Key Questions. He also realized that he needed to decide the correct number of clients Laura was going to be able to serve. Now, there was no random switching between salespeople, and this would ensure the building of a relationship. Laura would have information on what her clients liked and valued and most importantly what problems they need solving. It was Leo's answer to the Mackay 66 from Swim with the Sharks without being eaten alive. A book that influenced him tremendously.

He called Guy one more time to see if they could derive a logical number for Laura to have as her set number of customers.

Leo: "Hi Guy, me again, I hope you are well."

Guy: "Great as always Leo, I am glad you called, you will not believe my findings with my other B2B clients. They have the exact same situation as you guys in HAVCR Distribution have. There are 80% of their clients or more who buy very little, and the company never reaches out to them and does not even understand why they buy. They get a ton of calls and very little sales from these clients. So, I am going to use you as a guinea pig to see if your system works well. There is an interesting opportunity for many businesses to change their system, but first I want to see if it works with you."

They laughed.

Guy continued: "If it does work, would you give me more insight into the process to see if I dare implement it with those clients, obviously if you are ok with that?"

Leo: "Absolutely Guy, in many ways we are creating this together. The reason for my call is because I don't have an idea of how many people should this new salesperson handle. Is there a way to logically start with a good estimate?"

Guy: "Well, I remember when I was a consultant for a large national car dealership chain, they had a standard of 48 calls per salesperson per day. Each call had to be followed up by an email and the best salespeople also sent a text message."

Leo: "Ok, so that would be a bit of an overkill in our industry, we never want to be as pushy as car salespeople."

They both burst out laughing with that comment.

Leo: "Now, if they did 48, perhaps we can do 20 a day, since they will need to quote, follow up, listen, guide their customers, etc."

Guy: "Follow up, that is the golden rule that most salespeople never follow. My data shows that if we follow up 100% of our quotes, our closing ratio increases by 20%. That means, your system to proactively call customers, is backed up by real data. The beauty is that so many clients thank you for following up because they are so busy, they love it when you help them."

Leo: "I didn't like selling from the onset", yet I am becoming more passionate as I see the logic behind the numbers and make everything a process as a good Industrial Engineer would do. Now that you mentioned your experience with follow-up, I remember a comment made by a sales secretary during our weekly meeting. She explained that every quarter, at least, one customer complained about the lack of follow-up from the salesperson to their latest quote. I felt, are the shotguns being shot by the pigeons? That reality shows that we must include 100% follow-up of all quotes as part of the Moneycall system for sure."

Guy: "Great idea, but let's not lose track of the first question, how many customers shall the phone salesperson handle?"

Leo: "Right, so the Territory managers visit between 25 to 30 people a month, so the phone should be at least 4 to 5 times more productive, even if they must leave a message in a high percentage of cases. So do you feel like 100 is a good number to start?"

Guy: "That is a reasonable amount, and what would they say when they call"?

Leo: "I came up with the 5 Key Questions to understand what specifically the customer buys, and at the same time we need a script to make it easy for Laura to sell to her prospects the idea of providing information to her."

Guy: "That sounds like a great start to the system, what would be that opening script that you think could work magic?"

Leo: "We just need to keep things simple, so more or less like this: Mr Customer, I have been given your account to provide a more personalized service, I just need 17 minutes of your time, to ask some questions and understand how we can serve you better. Do you have time now so I can help you more?"

Leo continued: "The customer would then answer yes or no, if they say no, then we give them two alternatives on dates and times when we could have the conversation. If they say yes, we go into the first question right away. Bottom line when we get the "interview call" scheduled or accepted, we ask the 5Key Questions."

Guy:" That sounds easy enough, would love to see what results you get with it, and it sounds as it could work."

Leo: "Ok, so I am set to start my training with Laura on the 5Key Questions and will provide her with the first 100 clients that came after the top 20% in the Pareto analysis.

Guy: "Keep me posted, it sounds like a great plan. Now what I don't understand is what would you do after you got all the information from each customer? You need to call frequently or at least every month, so are you going to be asking the same questions all the time?"

Leo: "I remember that square that you taught us at the MBA which you learned from Joe Ellers, it showed the five ways you could increase your sales. Do you remember that?"

Guy: "Absolutely, that is a mind opener. Many salespeople think there are infinite ways to increase sales, if it was, then we could never get a handle on a process that would work. It helps to understand that quadrant."

Leo: "Well, I am working on using it for the following calls. I will tell you more about it later, I need to start training Laura on the new sales system and the 5 Key Questions, so she can be ready for opening day. See you later Guy."

Guy: "Stay in touch Leo, I truly like what I hear and the passion I see in you about this process".

They both went on to their respective activities feeling very excited about what they were creating.

Leo programmed his training with Laura and provided the 5 Key Questions to her and wanted to role play to make sure she felt comfortable with them and could ask confidently on her actual calls.

Leo: "Laura, you have the 5 Key Questions, and you are new to our organization, you never spoke to these clients before, so let's role play to make sure that you know how to handle the calls, does that make sense?"

Laura: "Sounds good. Shall I just ask you the first question?"

Leo: "Yes go ahead. Let's skip the intro selling the call and assume that you already had agreement from them, and they gave you 17 minutes. I will be the customer".

Laura: "Ok, here we go. Mr Leo, this is Laura with LATAM Supply, I hope you are well. As we agreed, we took the time today to see how we could serve you better. What would you say that you like about doing business with LATAM Supply?"

Leo (role playing as the customer): "Well Laura, I like it that you have very competitive pricing".

Laura: "Great, so now what do you like about" She did not get to finish, and Leo interrupted.

Leo: "Wait, wait, not so fast! The customer has not given you all the reasons why he likes to do business with us, so you must go deeper and never stop until the customer says, "and that is it" or something to that effect. Does that make sense?"

Laura: "Absolutely", she continued: "Mr Leo, I am glad that you like our prices, now what else do you like about doing business with us?"

Leo (as the customer role play): "I like that you provide a fast response to any warranty issue that I may have".

Laura: "Great, I am happy to hear that, many clients like that as well, what else would you say that you like?".

Leo (role playing): "I never have to worry about things not being ready when they are promised, so that saves me a lot of time and I like that from you guys."

Laura: "Great Mr Leo, saving time is certainly important, is there something else that you like?".

Leo: (role playing): "Nope, I can't think of anything else."

Laura: "Ok, so going to the next question, what is it about doing business with the competition that you like?"

Leo: "I love the fact that they never charge me a delivery fee no matter how big or small of a purchase I make".

Laura: "Well Mr Leo, if that is valuable to you, we can see how we can…. Leo interrupted again.

Leo: "What happens when you start explaining the shipping options we have?"

Laura: "He realizes we can do the same thing, but he also stops giving me information. . . I see your point Leo."

Leo: "Ok and how would you continue?"

Laura: "Interesting, zero delivery fee, what else do you like about doing business with our competitors."

Leo: "Well done, you did not stop the flow of information, so here I would say, (role play) I like their customer service."

Laura: "Customer service is key in any business relationship, besides customer service….." Leo interrupts one more time.

Leo: "Ok Laura, there are times when the customer will say things that require further clarification. This is a typical one, great customer service to you may be one thing and something very different to them. It is the customer's definition that we are after, so we need to clarify what he means by customer service.

Laura: "I didn't see it like that before and now I think it is a very interesting perspective."

Leo: "So how would you go about finding out their idea of customer service?".

Laura (going into her sales role): "Mr Leo, excellent service is key in any business relationship, could you tell me in more detail what does great customer service means to you?"

Leo: "Masterfully handled Laura! Consequently, I would answer: (role playing) I like the fact that they pick up the phone quickly for me or always call me back in less than 30 minutes. They also offer me their 24/7 concierge opening service, I truly appreciate that. Now another thing I like the most is that they always deliver on time."

Laura: "Great Mr Leo and what else do you like about doing business with them?"

Leo interrupted and said: "Laura, do you know what delivering on time means to him?"

Laura: "I see that I did not get that clarified. It's similar to the service question, I get it now!". She went on with her sales role again: "So, Mr. Leo, when you say that they always deliver on time what do you mean exactly?"

Leo: (role playing): "It means that if they say the equipment will be available in three days plus or minus two days, I know it is going to be five days max. So that is what I mean.

Laura (going back into her trainee role): "Now I see what you did there. Here, I understand what his standard is for being on time, my goal is to promise the same or better so we can get more of his business. I will do that on another call since my purpose is only to gather information at this time. Am I right?"

Leo: "You rock Laura, you will do great here for certain! Just make sure you write all his answers so you can use them on your follow-up call. I am glad that you remembered that this is not the time to offer on time delivery, we save that information for when we quote or when we promise him a delivery time."

Laura: "It's clear to me now: I am not selling; I am just getting information. The time to use that information will be in all my future calls".

Leo: "Super, that is exactly it." They fist-bumped.

Leo and Laura role played the 5 Key Questions several times, and the intro script for the call, the double alternative close to schedule the call, in case the customer did not have the time now. They even made "a ready to send text" that she would customize with the client's name, just to send to clients to pre-set the call and never surprise a customer nor make them feel interrupted.

Laura was now prepared for the first set of calls, yet they had two more weeks and Leo had to come up with the second part of the system for her follow-up calls through the whole year.

After thinking about the second part of the system for two days while Laura continued to practice her 5 Key Questions, Leo went back to the illustration that helped him a lot when it came to improving sales. It was taught to him by Guy and it came from a presentation by Joe Ellers in a trade association conference. He felt it had the basic idea of what they needed and showed it to Laura:

The five ways to increase sales

Increase the Price 5	Current Product/Service	New Product/Service
Current clients	1	2
Prospective clients	3	4

Source: Joe Ellers sales presentation in HARDI Focus Conference

Leo: "Hi Laura, I wanted to show this quadrant, so you can see that there are only a few ways to grow sales. We need to think about what questions we must ask using this quadrant for the follow-up calls with our clients. Proceeding in this manner, we can help the client and the company to sell more proactively. I also texted my old teacher, friend, and consultant Guy, who was the one who showed it to me, I will speak to him about it later, and I wanted to get your feedback on it first."

Laura: "I like that, yet it shows here that you have prospective clients and you said at first that we would not do prospecting, I am a bit confused there".

Leo: "I understand your concern, we will never do quadrant 4 in our industry, we would rely on marketing to produce leads for that. We have so much potential with all current clients who we are not presently serving well, that it makes no sense to focus on prospects. We need to concentrate our efforts in quadrants 1 and 2 because that is where most of our opportunities exist. It is so simple, to increase sales, we can see what products our current clients are no longer buying, which they used to buy from us, that is Quadrant 1. Then, we can also look at what they should buy from us and don't but today, that is quadrant 2. The key is how do we go about it? Please go home today and think it over, then let's get together again tomorrow to see how we will achieve it. It's that ok with you?"

Laura: "Ok. I will think on how to phrase questions for quadrants 1 and 2. I just need to keep in mind that the goal is to get information from the client, even in this new stage by asking, correct?"

Leo: "Exactly, the salespeople who ask the most questions, are the ones who sell the most. Just mentioning that fact, it started to give me some ideas on how to proceed. See you tomorrow and be ready to help me make something fantastic."

Laura smiled and they left to relax and be ready for the next day.

CHAPTER 5

THE SECOND PHASE OF THE MONEYCALL SYSTEM

Leo kept thinking about the questions and decided it was time to call Guy again to see what he thought and to share updates. After the regular personal and small talk, they got right into their conversation.

Leo: "Guy, as always needing to think out loud with you, so here I am with the situation that we talked about before, what do I do after completing the first calls with the 5KeyQuestions?"

Guy: "Leo, you got me thinking last time and I looked at the quadrant I taught you, as you requested, and several ideas came to mind. The first one is, since you are calling current customers, you already have data on what they buy don't you?"

Leo: "Yes, so what?" he replied, a little startled by his question.

Guy: "Well, how could you call your current clients about their latest purchases or their reasons for stopping buying a product so that is valuable to them?"

Leo: "Uhm Guy, I feel there is something interesting coming, yet I don't see it right now, tell me more."

Guy: "Well, current customers in quadrant 1:buy more of what they normally buy, buy again what they used to buy, or at least they give you information on why they stopped buying something that they used to buy. Since you have all their previous purchases in your system, the salesperson could make a personalized question about any of those situations, that will help the client and the company, right?"

Leo: "Wow! I like that idea, can we role play that possibility Guy? Do you mind? I would like to be the salesperson".

Guy: "Perfect, go for it".

Leo (role playing): "Mr Guy, as I told you before, I have been assigned to your account to give you a more personalized service. As I was making an analysis of your previous purchases, I noticed that you used to buy at least five 10 ton-packaged systems every month, yet in the last 3 months you have not purchased any of them, is there any reason for that?

Guy: "I like it, now that was something they stopped buying, what else could it be?"

Leo: "I could also ask about a projection of those units that they expect to buy in the next few months so we can ensure to have them in stock. I could ask about any product that they normally buy where timing would show they could be ready to get again. For example, I could say: Mr Guy, you normally buy five 10ton-packaged units on the 20th of the month, we are a couple of days to that, would you be making your regular order on that day so I can make sure that it is shipped, and you don't have to think about it?

Guy: "That's amazing! Now I can see how this proactive calling could be a game changer. If I was your customer, I certainly would like to have that level of service, certainly I would not call that selling, it is just helping me buy. Great thing Leo! Now how about the next quadrant?"

Leo: "Not so fast. I think we should always end any quadrant call with a modification of the question made famous by McDonalds: ""What else are you finding it hard to source these days that I could track down for you?

Guy: "I like that, it is a tried-and-true question, I can see how it adds value and it is easy for the customer and for the salesperson to ask. Now what about the second quadrant?"

Leo: "This is a bit trickier; we need to train the salesperson not only in how to search the system, but also to see what other products match the client's current purchases. I find it hard for customers to imagine blindly when they are asked if there were other products that they would include with their order. It opens their minds a lot more when we do the thinking for them and provide some obvious choices, don't you think so?"

Guy: "I guess it does, so for example if the carwash customer always buys car wax, then perhaps we can also offer them the tire shine liquid to make their tires look nice as well."

Leo: "Correct, I remember when I was a salesperson, a large portion of our clients did not buy many items simply because they did not know that we carried those products."

Guy: "Correct, I have found in my practice that clients also segment their sellers, so they think that they get car wax from store A but they think the tire shine liquid may only be found in store B. One day, you ask what other product they are having difficulty with, they mention tire shine and you say, we also have that. The customer about 90% of the time would mention, "I never knew you sold that item", and in the end it is because we are not proactive enough to ask. It's impossible for a customer to know all the 15,000 plus SKUs we carry."

Leo: "I agree, yet I also need to show Laura what products usually go together with other goods so she can easily ask the client about this other possibility."

Guy:" What would be your suggestion for her to handle that question?"

Leo: (went into role playing): "Mr Guy, I see that you always buy 1ton-mini splits from us every month, and you never carry the installation kits for them, they can save you a lot of time, have you ever tried one?"

Guy: "I like it, it is phrased in a simple but powerful manner to get valuable information. Now I think, you are ready to train Laura into the next stage of the system using the top 2 quadrants."

Leo: "I am super clear. Thanks, Guy, for pointing me in the right direction."

Guy: "My pleasure Leo, we are doing it together."

CHAPTER 6

GETTING READY TO ROLL

Leo went back to his role play with Laura and made sure that she knew the questions to ask, based on the top 2 squares of the quadrant and using their computer system to research the customer's previous orders before each call. Laura practiced for three days by herself in front of a mirror and with Leo until he felt she had a good handle on every type of call.

After Laura had practiced the scripts, she was very excited about starting to make calls and help clients buy. Her fear of making calls had totally disappeared since learning through role play for the past week. Now they were ready to roll and give the Moneycall system a try in the real world.

The store was stocked with products, the counter personnel was ready, the shipping and inventory people were set, it was all show time now! The marketing team had set up an opening ceremony, all the local customers that previously purchased from a further location were invited for the BBQ event. LinkedIn pics, invitation emails and videos, testimonials, brochures, vendors specials were announced. This was a huge kickoff for the inauguration of the branch.

The event rocked, it put the new location of LATAM Supply on the map. Customers were coming in and calling for orders, so it was business as usual rather soon. It was now time for Laura to try the new Moneycall system and see how effective it really was. She knew that for the system to be successful her sales had to be over $100,000 per month otherwise the productivity per employee of the store would be below the other stores.

Leo stayed close to her and listened to her first call on the 5 Key Questions. He loved it when Laura handled an interesting situation perfectly.

Laura: "Mr. Jones what is it that you like about doing business with LATAM Supply?"

Mr Jones (Customer): "I like the fact that you take care of my warranty issues really fast".

Laura: "I am glad that is important to you, now when you say we take care of warranty issues fast, what does that mean to you?"

Leo looked towards her giving her a thumbs up.

Mr. Jones: "Most of the time I get the part immediately after I bring it to you. If it is a big part, I know I will have it resolved in less than 2 working days, that is what you promise and you deliver on that promise. Nobody else does it better than LATAM Supply."

Laura: "Thanks for that explanation, Mr. Jones, we are glad you like that".

She continued to do that with all 100 of the clients assigned to her. She did have to leave voicemails, messages with secretaries, send texts, and emails to get the calls scheduled. Yet, she was clear in the overall objective "I am not selling, I am just getting information."

After about fifteen days, she had spoken to 63 clients. During the calls, many of them asked for products and she provided the answers and started to make sales. Some started to call her back and, in most cases, she also needed to make second calls and quote follow-ups.

Laura was great at using her CRM and she knew exactly who remained to be called, what they spoke about the last time and who qualified for the second phase of the system based on the quadrant.

Leo wanted to hear how her second set of calls would go. He sat next to Laura as she dialed Mr. Plum who liked products to be delivered on site and to get everything within 4 hours of his order, at the latest!

Laura: "Mr. Plum, how are you, it's Laura from LATAM Supply, how are you?

Mr. Plum: "I am well Laura, I am running to a new job, how can I help you quickly?"

Laura: "I was looking that you always buy copper pipes for your jobs, yet it has been more than 40 days since your last purchase, is there any reason for that?

Mr. Plum: "Wow! Actually, I need some pipes for the job I am currently doing and did not know we were low, thanks for letting me know, could you call me back in about 20 minutes when I get there and see how much we got left in the shop, so I can tell you exactly what I need?"

Laura: "Absolutely Mr. Plum, I can give you a call in 20 minutes, would this be a good number again?"

Mr. Plum: "Yes, please."

Laura: "Perfect, then please check to see if you need something else, and that way I can send you everything in one delivery this afternoon, is that fair enough?"

Mr. Plum: "That is super! You guys rock with this new service! Thanks Laura and keep up the good job."

Laura: "My pleasure Mr. Plum, talk to you later."

As Laura hung up the phone, Leo and she could not believe it. They were laughing and high-fiving from the comments of the customer. They felt they were on to something fantastic.

At the end of the month, when Leo got the sales numbers, they were climbing, day by day, even though they were behind the other stores in total sales, the start was the fastest on record of any store. Laura sold over $123,467 in her first month and was ahead of schedule.

Leo knew that he had a good system in place. He realized that he needed to get new salespeople on board to call the next batch of 100 local customers that LATAM Supply did not serve proactively. He was fortunate to start with a base of customers in his area, previously served from other locations. It was time to make these current customer sales grow instead of looking for new customers.

CHAPTER 7

LET'S SCALE IT!

Leo made up his mind quickly as he felt his Moneycall system shifting into high gear. Within 36 days of the grand opening, he hired 2 new salespeople and applied the same ideas that he had with Laura.

Leo felt it was a bit easier to train them as he not only used role-playing training, but he also had them listening to Laura making the actual calls. On average, she made thirty calls a day. Sometimes she could not get to talk to all of the clients she called, so she then left voicemails to those customers, along with an email and a text message. The scripts used were similar to this:

Mr. Customer, it's Laura from LATAM Supply. I got some information that might help you. Could you please call me back at 239-788-9003? If I don't hear from you, I will call you back on Wednesday. Talk to you soon, Laura.

It was all done rather quickly as she used the same template for all her messages. Normally, she received about5 calls back every day. Laura would talk to 10 to 15 people, make her quotes if she needed to, get feedback on deliveries, or send tech sheet information to her clients. She was a "busy bee", yet it never felt like she was selling. All she needed to do was to be proactive and to give value first.

Leo had the two new salespeople ready after their training. Tom and Maria were excited to work with real live customers after their 2-week training was complete. Leo was just as thrilled until the end of the month report showed him otherwise.

Maria made half the calls that Laura did. Tom made even fewer than Maria. Now when it came to sales, Maria was at $68,117 and Tom at $47,234. Leo was puzzled so he looked at the CRM. Tom had not filled the CRM with much information. When Leo looked further into the number of quotes and the percentage of closed business, Tom was at about 10%.

Leo needed to talk to his two new salespeople, and he felt that perhaps some of the problems with their results were his fault. He decided to call Guy one more time before he met with his personnel.

Leo: "Hi Guy, how are you?"

Guy: "Super Leo, I am waiting to hear the feedback from your sales system to see if I can implement it with my consulting clients that have recurring sales."

Leo: "Well, Laura is doing fantastic, she is selling more than $200K a month now, my issue is with the new people".

Leo's voice sounded disheartened.

Guy: "Wow! You got two more salespeople already; you surely move fast."

Leo: "Certainly the system is working, but now that I am scaling it, I am having some growing pains".

Guy: "Not everybody is doing as well as Laura is, am I right?"

Leo: "Yes, you're right. Their numbers are lower on calls, CRM usage, follow up on their quotes, in every metric, they are down, it does not make sense."

Guy: "Well then whose fault is it that they are not in the right place?"

Leo: "I know what you are going to say; I am the leader; it is my responsibility. However, I can't babysit them all the time, I need to say something to get them back on track. I just don't know what it should be?"

Guy: "When I hear, "I can't babysit them", I guess that you are having a monthly numbers meeting, is that right?"

Leo: "Yes, that is what we've always done at the company".

Guy: "Are you measuring results or are you measuring activities?"

Leo: "Hmmm, come to think of it, I was waiting for the results at the end of the month. Now come to think of it, those results come from the activities that the salespeople do every day."

Guy: "Right, less activities will yield less results, so if you look at the activities daily and weekly, then it will be easy to see if the results will be there, it makes sales predictable. Does that make sense?"

Leo: "Absolutely, I get it. I will have a daily 20-minute meeting to see the activities of the previous day and based on that I will take corrective action. I surely see that I need to pay more attention to Tom, and this idea sounds like a plan. It starts with me and in showing them how I will keep them on track."

Guy: "It is super important that you do that. Now as a sales manager, do you know what your main job is?"

Leo: "To get my people to produce results."

Guy: "Ok, sure, but what do you need to do to make sure that happens?"

Leo: "Here you go with your Yoda games."

Leo laughs as Guy remains quiet waiting for an answer. Leo thinks for a few minutes and Guy stays silent.

Suddenly Leo says: "I got it, my job is to guide them.

Guy: "Correct, show them where they are lacking, provide coaching by asking questions and help them plan for improvement. Your questions should assist them in deriving the plan by themselves."

Leo: "I like the results of your Yoda games, that is why I call you! From now on, this is exactly how I'll handle this situation. Thanks Guy."

Guy: "Talk to you soon Leo, keep me posted please".

As Leo returns to the office, he explains the situation to all three of the salespeople using a ranking system and how it's correlated to pay. This was something that also made the proactive Moneycall system more predictive: whoever makes more proactive calls also produces more sales and consequently more money. You can now predict the number of salespeople that you need to handle the amount of clients who bought regularly.

It is a mathematical equation: 1 salesperson to handle 100 Moneycall clients.

As Leo spoke to the team, Tom was surprised to see that by staying in his comfort zone he was making less money, and it was an eye opener for him. Leo made it completely clear when he posted the numbers and sales results that if you make more calls, talk to more people, and follow-up more, you will make more money and the numbers clearly already showed that.

Calls   Quotes   Follow-ups

Laura	380	157	At 100% of quotes
Maria	177	53	At 67% of quotes
Tom	102	19	At 42% of quotes

From the numbers Leo made it clear that Laura was making about 4 times more calls than Tom was, and he surely got the message. Still all the numbers helped the new location have higher sales per employee metrics, but Leo knew he was on to something big here.

After a month, all the salespeople had better results. Obviously, Laura improved the least as she was doing rather well and following up 100% of her quotes, so it looked like the new management system, with frequent sales meetings and coaching, was also providing better guidance for them.

Another key metric was that the salespeople should expect to provide about 50% of quotes from their calls. If that number is lower is because they were not making enough square 2 quadrant calls or not detecting enough products that are no longer being purchased in square 1. As all salespeople understood that the Moneycall system was the key to getting more sales results, more and more salespeople started to follow it.

With all the recent success, Leo knew that he needed to shift his attention to the ordering, logistics and inventory side of the business since he was going to run out of products quickly. Sales were coming in faster than their most optimistic numbers and even as it was a good problem to have, he knew that without products his people could not produce sales results.

Luckily, Leo was able to talk to his father, who had been quietly following the sales ramp up from Leo's location. He was extremely proud and happy with the results thus far. Because of this attention to detail, he had already moved certain things around with his logistics team so that Leo's worry was already addressed. At least for the moment.

CHAPTER 8

TIME FOR THE BIG STAGE

After six months, Leo kept on growing until he had taken care of all the customers in the list and assigned them to a salesperson. 1,500 customers now had a proactive Moneycall salesperson assigned to them, and some of those customers had increased the amount of business with the new location at LATAM Supply up 10-fold with an average of 20%increase in revenue. Now they had 15 salespeople at the new department, yet it was time for the next big step.

Leo knew that once an account was at $60,000 per year or more, he needed to assign it to a territory Manager who could provide even more personalized service by visiting the client in person.

A dedicated territory manager could also:

1) Make a more individualized plan for growth

2) Provide a training schedule

3) Plan different options for coop marketing

4) Arrange for guidance with certain complex projects.

It was time to promote Laura to Territory Manager (TM) and her job was to visit 25 clients in person every week. Leo took the biggest clients of all 15 Moneycall salespeople and a few from the other TMs who had over 25 and assigned them all to Laura.

Leo asked one of the most experienced TMs to help train Laura on what to do during each visit: What questions to ask, how to bring new trends from the industry and to become an advisor to her 25 customers. The objective was never to sell, but rather to help her clients increase their business. She did that by planning, making sure her clients priced their services correctly, providing ideas for their marketing, and looking for profitable niches that they could exploit. The key is to understand that for her to be successful she needed to help her customers in those areas where they could do better. Most contractors are great at installing, fixing, and maintaining equipment; however, they are not so good at keeping good business records, marketing, selling solutions vs just price, customer service, asking for referrals, that is why many of them don't make it over the long haul.

Laura learned her lesson well during her time working on the phones. Leo was there to provide support and her new 25 customers loved the attention and the proactive care that they received from her and from LATAM Supply.

That same process would be repeated every time the company would get another Moneycall customer to buy $60,000/yr or more. That number could be adjusted in other locations, yet for now that was the cutoff number that made sense for them based on the analysis of total sales per the top 20% of clients. That is what LATAM Supply sales departments called: The big time.

CHAPTER 9

IF YOU MEASURE IT, THEY WILL GROW WITH I³

Guy had been keeping an eye on the results that Leo and his team were getting at LATAM Supply as he found that his other distributor clients were in a very similar situation. They were reactive in their sales process, customers always called, their marketing was geared towards generating customer calls and their process was set up to take care of those calls quickly, yet never fully understanding what problems the customer really needed to solve. One of the reasons is that when customers called, many times they were handled by a different person; the system was set up to reduce wait time, not to increase customer service quality or personalization. Guy had a numerical, statistic a land a procedural mind, so Leo got him thinking long and hard about this Moneycall proactive system. It made total sense to him since he was always thinking about his recurring sales customers in distribution and manufacturing.

Now Guy wanted to implement the same process with those clients, but he needed to understand more in depth and how Leo measured the KPIs of the process. So, he decided to call Leo.

Guy: "Hi Leo, I hope you are well, how is everything going?"

Leo: "Hey Guy, good to hear you again, it is going great, we are set to be the branch with the fastest sales growth ever out of the other 17 locations. And if we keep it up, perhaps I can win the challenge with my old man and have the system implemented in all locations."

Guy: "That is great to hear Leo, I am calling you for precisely for that same reason. You know that I was always interested to see the results that you would get with your implementation. I also wanted to make sure there was a repeatable process that I could apply with my other clients. Now I believe what Peter Drucker said, "If you don't measure it, you can't manage it", therefore I imagine that you must have some key KPIs to make sure that things run smoothly, is that right?"

Leo: "You are right Guy, without KPIs we could not get the I^3, which are: *Improve* current results, *Increase* productivity and *Identify* potential areas of improvement or where some salespeople did better than others so we can copy best practices. Those 3 things can only be obtained by measuring the whole process daily."

Guy: "I love it Leo, could you describe the whole process for me so I can replicate it with my other clients?"

Leo: "Sure, you have been involved since the beginning so you may remember it is all based on numbers. Here it is:

1) Make an 80/20 analysis to determine which customers you will call first and start with one salesperson and let the success take you from there. You will pick the 80% who do not buy as much from you as the 20% who call frequently and like doing business with you regularly. Remember "*your best customers want to*

be your customers, and your "not so good customers" prefer to buy from the competition", so you need to serve them better and differently to get more business from them. Those are our first targets with the proactive Moneycall system."

Guy: "I see, what else."

2) You later use a script to sell the 5 Key Questions call, sometimes it is great to send a text first to coordinate it, this is even better during low season so customers can give you more of their time. The key to the script is "Mr Customer, I was given your account in order to provide a more personalized service to you and your company, may

you give me 13 minutes to ask you a few questions to serve you better?". And the objective of the call is to understand "What they buy" and here you ask the 5 basic questions which you already know:

1) Why they like to do business with us,
2) Why they like doing business with the competition
3) What % of what they buy they buy from us
4) What they are having issues finding
5) What niche of the market they would like to penetrate and have not been able to do yet.

If they had dealt with the salesperson before we would add a 6th question:

6) what do you like about doing business with me?

Leo replied: How does that sound so far Guy?"

Guy: "Makes total sense, I remember the questions and that the key was not to stop asking for what else they like until the customer says, that is it. I feel it is a mini "market research" which is a great way to start any business venture, what else is there?"

Leo: "It is important that you keep track of what the customers say that they like in your CRM or at least an excel sheet so that every time that you interact or quote them, these are considered and included in the proposal since that is what they value and makes you different."

Guy: "That is very logical, now do you keep track of any KPIs?"

Leo: "Yes, that is what comes next, we must measure everything to get the I^3, keep in mind, we never give them a list of more than 100 clients, and these are the only customers they call upon or get calls from.

Here are the KPIs that we track in the new Moneycall department:

1) "**Amount of outgoing calls** made by each salesperson (we look for 20 to 30 per day per salesperson). We log them as S1 or S2 for square 1 or 2 of the sales quadrant questions. We are not doing S3 for now, yet we are open for that later. S4 is another monster, and it requires more marketing involvement and for our type of recurring sales, we don't need as much as other industries as we already spoke about."

2) "**Number of calls received** (we look for a ratio of 80% outgoing to 20% incoming to make sure we are truly proactive). If the calls are return calls, we log them as S1 or S2 depending on the preparation the salesperson made when they called. If they call asking for help on a particular item or situation, then we log it as an incoming call. We then always end up with the McDonalds question. "What else would you like today?" They both smiled at that, knowing it made sense.

3) "We also look at **how many quotes were made per salesperson**; we expect a quote to be requested on 50% of the calls. If the customer has already set pricing with us, we

remind them what that is and they either place the other right there, or if they don't decide immediately we ask for a date that the customer feels they will have a decision, for the seller to follow up the quote."

4) "The number of quotes led us to measure our **Closing Ratio** at the end of the month in 2 ways:
a) Number of quotes made divided by quotes closed.

b) Total dollar amount quoted divided by total sales in dollars."

Guy interrupted: "Leo, why measuring closing ratio in those 2 different ways"?

Leo: "Great question Guy, the reason is that we want to see if there is a lot of discrepancy in the two numbers, which would indicate that we are winning on the small dollar amount more than the large dollar amount or vice versa. Now, if the numbers are rather similar, we know there is no real difference. We expect a closing ratio of at least 20% and there should not be a difference of more than 5 percentage points between the 2 closing ratio calculations. Does that make sense?"

Guy: "Absolutely, please keep going with the KPI's"

5) Leo continued: "One of the most important KPIs is: **Follow-up to quotes. First, I recommend that all the Follow-ups are recorded into the CRM. But, for the plan to work best, I suggest you use** two different types: follow-up call 1 (F1) and 2 (F2), let me explain before you get confused. We want to have everyone follow up their

quotes 100% of the time, and that is to make sure the customer has it, understands it and provides a feedback date. Sometimes the customer orders at F1, in our business, we get the order 60% of the time at that stage, so you can see the importance to doing that call. Now the other 40% of the time our goal is to get a feedback date from the customer. At that time, we want to follow up again and see if they decided to order or not. Sometimes we get the order, sometimes we don't and sometimes we do not even get a response. For that reason, we have follow-up call 2 (F2), we expect 100% of F1calls and at least 50% on F2. And from the 50% of F2 we expect at least

50% or 25% of all quotes to be a sale. Right now, we are closing at a minimum of 25% of our quotes and the trend is increasing. By making the 5Key Questions we are showing more value outside of price to our customers and we are above the closing ratio of the whole company. We noticed that by just making these calls, our closing ratio increased by 25% from 20% at the beginning of the year to the 25% we have now, and we have the highest closing ratio of any location in the company. Plus, I see that ratio trending higher bit by bit. Am I making myself clear?"

Guy: "Absolutely, that is a great idea with the Follow Up (F calls) and the results speak for themselves, please continue."

6) Leo continued:

"We make our **Delivery Call**(DC) which is a call after each delivery or pickup order from "Will Call" at the store. Our objective is to make sure that everything is received as planned and to reassure the customer that they can count on us. It is a great time to celebrate and hear great things about what we do and get on the good side of the client. After 10 straight calls with 100% satisfaction on delivery or pickup of their orders then we have the next call that we measure. Of course, that should go into the CRM as well.

Guy: "Interesting, what is that other call type you measure?" he asked while being a bit surprised about how detailed the process had become since Leo and him started talking.

7) Leo continued:

"10 straight (DC) leads to the **Referral Call** (RC) here the objective is to say that we are happy that they find our service valuable for their business and if they would be willing to refer us to someone who could also benefit from our service. After we get an answer, we ask to see if an email introduction would be ok with them. 30% of the time we get the email yet when we offer to send them an email summarizing what they said and making the presentation with "the person they named" where they only need to approve the email and put the name of the person and signature, we get a higher number, sometimes as close as 70%.

Guy: "Wow that is impressive, I have never seen this so systematic!"

Leo: "That is the key in being PROACTIVE and having us in control of the process by measuring every step."

Guy: "What happens with the ones that prefer not to provide any referrals?"

Leo: "Our plan B for those is to always ask for a short 20 second video testimonial. We later post them on our social media pages and on LinkedIn. Those videos always end up providing more business and even help our "in-person visit salesperson or TM" when they are trying to get a new contractor onboard.

Guy: "Great, now I understand why I see so many video testimonials from your customers on LinkedIn, yet surely not all provide the videos as well. What do you do then?"

Leo: "Remember Guy that we had ten straight DC (delivery/pickup calls) with 100% satisfaction with them at this point, so we have earned the right to ask, now it is true, some say they can't think of anyone to refer to us or can't do the video as they are on a rush all the time, for those we wait for 5 more DC calls with 100% satisfaction to go to our plan C. We proceed here to simply summarize what they said and get it approved by them. Afterwards, we use it on our webpage or social media along with many others. In short, when we have earned the right to a testimonial, we do our best to get one. What I found is that people do not feel bad to be asked if you have delivered first. I rarely got a negative response because we served first; we had a clear plan A, then immediately a plan B and after 5 more DC calls a plan C. Sure we get people who still do not comply after using all 3 plans, but in my experience this system reduces those situations to about 10% or less vs more than 70% with any other method that I studied. For that reason, referral calls are our KPI number 7. We give those potential customers to our experienced TM's and they decide if the starting volume makes sense for them or if it is smaller for the Moneycall department."

Guy: "Impressive Leo, great job with that system, I love referrals and video testimonials are the best. Any other KPI that you measure?"

8) Leo continued:

"We recently added a new KPI that we learned from a book by Alex Goldfayn which is to call customers just to see how they are, no business in mind, just to truly know about the person. We call these Personal Touch (PT) calls. We also have tickets for ball games, we encourage our people to go out with our customers and have lunch plus we also do our hot dogs BBQs frequently. Every time we do not see a customer for a while, we try to get to see them outside of work. It is a personal touch, it is not business, it is not required, but at least we want to have that PT call. We expect our salespeople to make those at least once a quarter. So, our PT call is our KPI number 8 yet the number does not mean that it is 8th in importance, it is just another KPI to measure.

Guy added: "Looking good so far, anything else?"

9) Leo:

"There is another KPI that helps us measure how much confidence we are building with our contractors. This is a result of the Moneycall system, it does not measure the day-to-day success of it, yet it measures the long-term partnership that we are building with our contractors. We look at what percentage of our contractors allow us to help them with their final customers on projects of more than $50,000. We know that if the distributor and the contractor get involved together the closing ratio increases by 50% and if the equipment manufacturer and the distributor come together with the contractor the closing ratio increases by 65%. For that reason, we track that percentage in our start of the year calls, so this is not a monthly ratio to measure. Doing this type of call at the beginning of the year sets the tone with our customers to keep us in mind if they have a big project. We know contractors need all the help in selling that they can get; sometimes they are afraid of being "too expensive" and we must help them sell a solution to a problem and never a product. I remember well, if you sell products, you sell price, if you sell solutions to problems, you sell with profits."

"Absolutely I am glad you learned that well, when you sell products you sell price, and I agree, to start the year with those calls to contractors is a great idea." replied Guy.

Leo   mentioned:

10)"Lastly, we track opportunity size, we look to see how big a particular quote is and if we need to get more people involved to help the client close a deal. Sometimes, engineering needs to help, sometimes a sales manager needs to get involved because the size of the deal requires it. To detect those situations, we look at the size of the deal. Our rule is, if it is more than $10,000, we meet to see if more support needs to be provided to make sure the customer gets the deal. Our goal is to be proactive serving, never reactive.

Guy: "Wow! I see that you guys are serious about being proactive at every level. That is amazing."

Leo: "This last point ties well with the previous % who is willing to introduce to us the final customer. Because it is easier to offer help on a $10k deal to a customer who already said they are open for us to help them, than when you have a customer who prefers to handle those opportunities on their own."

Guy: "I can see that better now, having the information surely improves sales results. It's certainly better to be proactive in getting the information."

Leo: "**We want to be on offense never on defense**, it is too late by the time we react, plus it gives us a clear differentiation strategy to our competitors.

The number of clients that have decided to do more business with us has increased and we get positive feedback all the time. Thanks to our salespeople being on top of things, we frequently hear our clients saying: "I forgot about this, you saved me with this call", and more along those lines. Our job is more fun, yet it requires more planning and a smooth operational process so that our sales efforts do not fall by the wayside. Remember *"having the product increases your probability of selling it"*. It all follows the formula: **Max sales=Structure x System x Operations**.

We have the right structure and the right system now and we need to also make sure that the warehouse, accounting, purchasing, inventory control and logistics do their job as well. We all need to be on the offensive never on the defensive."

Guy: "I love that sales formula, where did you get that?

Leo: "I came up with it, I needed to understand what had to come first and how each part of the system impacted everything else."

Guy: "Very interesting, I just hope the formula is not too complex, remember that I want to implement the system with other clients.

Leo: "For those clients that are just looking to implement the Moneycall system, there is a more simplistic formula that we can cover later."

Guy: "Great, could you give me some more detail on the formula as you have it now and then we can see the simplified version?"

Leo: "Sure. Structure is to have all bases covered in our sales structure: counter, inside sales, Moneycall sales, TM sales and internet sales. The 80/20 rule will let you know the number of clients that each department has to handle in order to be effective. Since the Counter is reactive, it will depend on the store visits and not by the number of clients. All other departments must start with the clients that our 80/20 analysis mandated. The base should be: 100 clients for the Moneycall department and 25-30 for the Outside sales department. And we must have the right people on each seat as they say. The sales manager is 70% of the equation, so if the sales manager is doing 100% of the "guiding to the salespeople, he would score 1 if he is doing 70% he would score 0.7. The other 30% comes from the people in each department doing everything correctly with their customers. In the Moneycall department, we look for them to pass with at least 80% on their scripts, role playing and system research by customer, before we have them making calls."

Guy: "So for your Structure to be 100% you would have the sales manager doing 100% of coaching, call controlling and guiding x 70% of the equation. To that, you add your salespeople that passed a test for role playing, using scripts, and researching in the system what the customer ordered before for S1 calls or what they need to add to future orders or S2 calls and multiply that by 30% for the second part of the equation. Right?"

Leo: "Correct Guy"

Guy: "Ok, so let's say your structure is 100%, now what?"

Leo: "Just imagine that you have Structure at 100% and System at 100%, this is a multiplication so if operations is at 70%, you would have: $1 \times 1 \times 0.7 =$ 70% of maximum sales capacity. It just shows you how hard we must work in every part of the equation to be over 90% at least."

Guy: "I see now, please go on".

Leo: "In System, we look for each salesperson using the KPIs and ranking at 100% in each, obviously some will rank less, yet that shows them what they can improve. For example, if they make the right number of calls (20-30), make 50% of the calls into quotes, follows up each quote F1 and then F2 is at least 50% then they would score 100% in each of those 4 which makes 25% of the System equation.

Guy: "Ok, let me see if I get it for the System part of the equation. Here there are 4 parts, if the salespeople make 100% of the calls, they get a 1 or 100% and then we look at number of quotes, if it is less than 50%, let's say 40% they score 0.8 or 80%, then follow up calls F1, if they do 92% they get 0.92 and if they do less than 50% of FU2, let's say 45% they get a 90% or 0.9."

Leo: "That is correct, now how would it look in simple math?"

Guy: "Using the previous numbers, then it would be:

# of calls 100% x quotes 80% x F1 92% x F2 90%

=

1 x 0.8 x 0.92 x 0.9

=

0.66 or 66%.

Wow! That shows me the importance of getting everybody onboard with the system. According to this you would score 66% on the System variable."

Leo interrupted: "Correct Guy, it pushes you to make sure that you get the most out each player when it comes to the KPIs."

Guy: "Now how would the Operations variable be calculated in order to get the whole equation in place?"

Leo: "This one is trickier because you have 4 components yet "on time delivery" takes 90% of the equation. The reason is, that if you do not deliver on time at a high percentage of the customers, you are done in this business."

Guy cuts in saying: "No Leo! in any business, you need to deliver on the day that you promised, not just in yours."

Leo: "Correct Guy, so that is why it is at 90%, please keep in mind that we also measure here what percentage of what we promised was delivered on time, so if we promised 10 parts and 5 got there on time, we are at 50%."

Guy: "That is so logical!".

Leo: "Then you have 3 other variables. The first one is Account Receivables (AR): If customers are paying above industry standards, you make it 100% and deduct a proportion depending on how far away you are. Then, if your AR is at 35 days and the industry standard is 30 you are 5/30=17% less efficient, so your number would be 100%-17% = 83%. Makes sense to you?"

Guy: "The math makes sense but why are you using AR as an operational metric?"

Leo: "I put accounting, purchasing, warehousing, delivery, all into operations, because if they fail, my sales will be negatively impacted and more costly. Therefore, AR shows the level of customers' satisfaction with our company and how much they prefer to pay us first vs other suppliers. Plus, it also indicates that a higher AR generates more expenses, especially with higher interest rates. In the end if your customer is not paying on time, we are not proactive enough and we need to see how to change that before it gets out of hand."

Guy: "I feel it is an interesting idea, tell me about the other variables just to get a better feel for everything."

Leo: "The second variable is: Customer Service Ranking (CSR). This is a great measure to understand how our operations produce the service our customers expect.

And finally, the third variable is: Invoice Discrepancies (ID). We need to measure what percentage of discrepancies- price, product, quantity etc... from the initial documentation to the final invoice, we made. This percentage shows how much friction the whole operations have created for the customer to be satisfied. If 3 of 300 invoices or a 1% error was made in a period, then we would get a 99% on that variable."

Guy: "Let me do the math here: 95% on time delivery (OTD) would be 90% or 0.9 of the equation, then if AR is 17% off the benchmark, we would be at 83%, if Customer Service Ranking (CSR) was at 4 out 5 we would be at 80% and if Invoice Discrepancies had a failure rate of 1% we would be at 99%.

So, the math is:

Variable 1

OTD = 95% = 0.95

Variables 2-3-4:

AR = 83% = 0.83

CSR = 80% = 0.80

ID = 99% = 0.99

Now, I remember that you mentioned that OTD explains 90% of the equation and the 3 other variables the remaining 10%. In simple math, it would look like this:

Variable 1

0.95 x 0.9 = 0.86

Variables 2-3-4:

(0.83 x 0.80 x 0.99) x 0.10 = 0.066

The total for the Operational Variable is:

0.86 + 0.066 = 0.926 = 93%

Leo: "Great, so now you have 100% on Structure x 66% in system x 93% in Operations. That means in this particular example,that your maximum sales percentage would be: Estructure 1 x System 0.66 x Operations 0.93= 61% so you are selling about 60% of what you could sell. Imagine what would happen if you improved all the metrics in the equation?"

Guy: "I see clearly that if we make small improvements in each of those areas in the equation, we can get gigantic leaps in sales results."

Leo: "That is exactly what has happened, yet as you can see from what the calculation shows, any company could benefit by using that Max Sales formula and improving in each of its steps."

Guy: "I totally get it, the numbers show where we need to improve, but are those your real numbers?"

Leo: "No, our numbers have improved since we started. Our branch of LATAM Supply is currently at 100% x 89% x 91%= 81%. We must improve still, right now I am concentrating more on the sales system, later I will look at the other areas a bit deeper. The key is that I have more control of the sales system as Sales are my responsibility. I must delegate the other areas to my team, yet I know that I need to give them support as well."

Guy: "Absolutely, you can't do everything at the same time. Now on another subject with the calls, to clear all this math from my head a bit. Did you ever get an angry customers not wanting to be called, especially in this age of texting?"

Leo: "Nobody ever gets angry for following-up, particularly when you are providing a personalized service. We earn the right to call them back after quoting or giving requested information. We always agree to the call on text, especially the first call with the 5 Key Questions, from there we agree on monthly or bi-weekly calls to provide individualized service and they choose the best time and day for those calls. If they want us to coordinate it by text, we, do it, yet the key is to talk to the customer with something meaningful to ask or to say and if nothing else to say hello on a PT call."

Guy: "I would have expected to get more negative reactions, and this is surprising to me".

Leo: "It is interesting that you say that because many of our salespeople believed the same thing at first. In reality, when you call to serve and not to sell and when you ask a simple question based on the analysis of the buying patterns of our clients, they truly appreciate what we do. Nobody else does it and it makes us stand out."

Guy: "I want to implement it for sure, I will take your KPIs and process to digest it. Perhaps I could see it in action at your place if you don't mind and then see how I can help my clients with it. It would be interesting to see if they have the data to calculate the Maximum Sales with your equation. Yet for sure I want to see you guys in action. I also would like to call you in a few days after I digest all the formula, to see the simplified version, if that is ok with you Leo."

Leo: "It would be my pleasure Guy, one last thing before you hang up, keep in mind, the salespeople that insist on texting, never do as well as the ones who call. We found that many just love to text all day long and texting is truly in vogue now, yet you will never be able to get the amount of information by text only. The most successful salespeople used text to coordinate calls or to ask permission to call and reduce the number of texts and even the possibility of misunderstandings. So, keep an eye on that."

Guy: "Great tip Leo, nothing is as good as the experience of the person implementing the process. Thanks for the trust and the feedback."

Leo: "My pleasure Guy, I am sure it will make us improve our process as well to hear your feedback and best practices achieved with your clients in the future."

Guy: "That sounds like a plan. Let me digest all this information and then I will coordinate my next call with you on the simplified formula. I also want to visit your location so I can see everything working at your place".

Leo: "Perfect, talk to you soon Guy."

CHAPTER 10

A SIMPLIFIED APPROACH TO LEO'S SALES FORMULA

As Guy had promised, he was looking deeper into the sales formula that Leo shared with him. Guy loves analysis and making decisions based on facts.

Yet the key to him was to find the point of view of the clients into implementing the system and the formula.

After talking to several of his clients, Guy found that most of them did not have the data needed to make the full analysis that the formula from Leo required. From that feedback he understood that the key is to get started, especially if there was a simpler way to do it.

Like always, Guy scheduled his call with Leo to see the simplified version for those distributors that are just getting started.

As the day of their call arrived Guy was looking forward to what Leo had to say

Guy: "Hi Leo, thanks for taking the time with me today to talk about the simplified version of the formula that you told me about."

Leo: "Surely Guy, I am glad that you are taking the formula and the system so seriously. As you can imagine, I did not get to where we are today immediately, we grew from the simple idea of looking to become proactive. The basic principle is not just that 20% of your clients give you 80% of your sales, but most importantly that 20% of your activities produce 80% of your results. So, the Moneycall system looks to focus your efforts into that 20% of your efforts that gives you the best results. That is how we began the whole process."

Guy: "I never actually stopped to think about that side of the Pareto principle, but it also makes sense that 20% of your activities should produce 80% of your results. Don't keep me in suspense, tell me how to start in a simpler way".

Leo: "The formula itself is the same, yet the parameters to look for in each are much less and for that same reason simpler."

Guy: "Ok, so it is still Structure x System x Operations= Maximum Sales, is that right?"

Leo: "Yes, now in Structure the key is that you look to see if you have a specialized sales channel structure for each sales type. So, most distributors would have a: Counter, Inside Sales (general incoming sales calls), Moneycall (proactive outgoing sales calls to assigned customers), outside sales (TM sales) and Internet."

Guy: "Nothing new there so far"

Leo: "Now, you must have the correct and specialized people in at least two of the four channels. Some distributors do not have a counter department, most distributors do, but the key is that at least two of those must specialize in what they do and must be focused in the right amount of clients to not waste their 20% most productive effort."

Guy: "Could you give me an illustration to understand it better?"

Leo: "Sure, Let's say that your client has a counter and has an Outside sales department. The counter taking calls is not really a telephone sale, that is still 100% reactive so it counts as a counter sale, it was just made on the phone. Now that is the way counter sales work, so that is OK. Now, if the Outside sales department has more than 30 clients per salesperson then that is an issue, you will not be able to visit all your clients if you try to cover too many with a salesperson. By covering too many clients you will lose the opportunity to serve and understand those clients more and part of the most valuable 20% effort will be wasted looking for less profitable clients."

Guy: "Now how do you define which is your 20% activity for a salesperson?"

Leo: "Beautiful question Guy, would you care to take a chance on the answer?"

Guy: "Well, I would say anything related to being in front of a customer or at least talking to the customer."

Leo: "That is 100% right, your most important activities as a salesperson is to talk to the customer, and my other question would be, who is a customer?"

Guy: "The person or company that buys from you, isn't it?"

Leo: "Yes and the one that buys more often is more of a real customer in a recurring sale industry than those that buy once a year. Therefore, our goal is to have the most amount of time possible in front of those customers who do most business with us. We find that more contractors want to do business with us if we understand them more and if we solve their problems, we can only gain that knowledge by being close to them. That is why it is so important to have the right number of clients per each sale channel in our company."

Guy: "Ok, so here structure means the amount of people each department has to handle, so we can concentrate the effort of each salesperson into what produces the most bang for the buck, correct?"

Leo: "Could not say it any better myself. They both laughed.

Guy: "Super, now I make sure that 2 departments are well staffed and concentrated 100% on their duties with their correct amount of clients, where does the system part come in?"

Leo: "System starts with **proactivity**."

Guy: "Ok, again give me an example of that"

Leo: "Sure, let's say that you got your first person for the Moneycall department and that salesperson has been assigned 100 clients that were underserved as per your 80/20 analysis. If that person takes more calls than the ones made, then you have an issue. The whole purpose of the system is to make sure that we are proactive, so the sales manager must see if his new salesperson is making at least 80% of the calls that they handle. Rule #1 is: Moneycall will work if we are making calls according to the system that I described before, if in the end we take more calls than we make, the sales manager is not guiding the system correctly because that is a reactive system not proactive."

Guy: "But Leo, most of the inside sales departments work in taking calls all day long and that works for all the companies that I know."

Leo: "It works to keep the current clients that prefer you and are happy enough with you, but it does not allow you to serve all your customers as well as you could. Inside sales, the way it is done today is reactive, the customer starts the process and the salesperson must react with their needs."

Guy: "I see it now, by changing the nature of the call from reactive to proactive you must also increase the amount of people calling so you can help your clients with what they are not looking at right now, correct?"

Leo: "Yes, but that part scares business owners, yet if you think of only adding one person at the time, and waiting for the results to show that it makes sense to add another, then it is easier. Plus, it helps to ramp up slowly at first since you need to train each person that starts the Moneycall system."

Guy: "I get it, this is a lot easier to manage to begin with, I can see why it is a simpler version, yet it is still not an easy task."

Leo: "If it was easy, everybody would be doing it. Salespeople are like water, they will look for the easiest way out, our job is to guide them to make sure that the system is respected. I found that when we show the 80/20most salespeople will see that they are stretched too thin into too many clients that are not in their top 20%. Actually, when you ask them: who is your client #11? They will not know, because most of them don't rank them."

Guy: "That means that when you show them those clients that produce the biggest results, they are willing to concentrate better."

Leo: "Yes, for your Moneycall Salesperson, when you hire or promote from another department, they are more likely to be open to this new idea of handling fewer clients. I would not recommend promoting a counter salesperson or an outside salesperson (Territory Manager TM) to this position. The reason is that the DNA of a Moneycall salesperson must be proactive, they have to be the ones initiating the conversation and they must have something of value in each interaction on the phone. It is highly unlikely that a Counter person does that, and a TM will probably see it as a negative promotion and certainly will affect their commission schedule."

Guy: "I see, so System, in the simplified version is making sure we are serving the right number of clients, and we are proactive except of course in the Counter, for those distributors that have it."

Leo: "That is perfect"

Guy: "Great, so what about the Operations side of the formula?"

Leo: "You will love this, because the Structure and System will take a lot of time and effort, and most established companies need to have decent operations otherwise they would not survive. So just concentrate on the first two and don't worry about operations until you have the rest of the KPIs ready to be measured. So, concentrate on getting the structure and the system right, meaning the right people specializing on one type of sales system with the right number of clients and being proactive on everything but on Counter Sales and you will be on your way."

Guy: "Yup, I love it, that is simple enough to get started."

Leo: "It is simple, yet that does not mean it is easy" ......They both laughed.

Guy: "I know, like you would say, if it was easy, everybody would be doing it, yet it is simple to understand, and I can see my clients being open to start with at least one person in their Moneycall department."

Leo: "Super, that is what you should strive for, to get one person with 100 clients assigned to that salesperson asking the right questions and with the right DNA for being proactive."

Guy: "Have you found a type of person that works better to start the Moneycall department?"

Leo: "Yes, anybody coming from a phone sales background where they had to do prospecting, even if we do not prospect, we do need to be conversation starters. In that regard we exchange prospecting for understanding and reaching out to our current customers vs new potential clients. A second possibility is a person from the warehouse who wants to get into sales, if they are truly hungry and willing to try new things, they could also be great since they know a lot of the products."

Guy: "I understand your logic, it's good to get feedback from your experience, it will make my job easier with my clients, thanks Leo."

Leo: "My pleasure Guy, do you feel that you have a better grip on the simplified version of the formula?"

Guy: "Actually, I think I have a better understanding of the whole system now that we have narrowed down the essentials to get the wheels turning. Is there anything else that you would like to add before we end our call?"

Leo: "Yes, you cannot overlook the importance to have a strong sales manager who is tough on having the system respected yet is also a great coach and is aware that things will take time."

Guy: "I see, it is an interesting combination for a sales manager, most of them are too soft or too afraid of their salespeople, yet to be firm and also a good coach is an interesting combination. I can see why you have so much weight in the formula for the sales manager."

Leo: "Absolutely Guy, the sales manager is the key into getting the system implemented correctly. The manager must understand the system well and must know how to implement it and coach it along the way to get the right results."

Guy: "It's all much clearer to me now, thanks for making things simpler for me. If you think about it, at the beginning, I will be like the sales manager for my clients in order for them to implement the system."

Leo: "Correct, you need to train either a sales manager or a salesperson for each of your clients, so you must explain the system and coach them along the way to get the results."

Guy: "I feel more comfortable with the system now, yet I want to see it in action, because I will be the one making sure that it is implemented with my clients. This call was certainly very valuable for me to understand everything better."

Leo: "I am glad you feel that way. Now let me know when you want to see our guys working in the office so you can see the whole thing in operation."

Guy: "I will review my previous notes on the complete formula and the KPIs and will coordinate that visit with you, no worries, I am truly excited to see it working".

Leo: "All right, so I will wait for your call then."

They both exchanged niceties and agreed to coordinate the visit that Guy knew would help him understand everything so much better.

CHAPTER 11

THE DISH TASTES BETTER IN THE KITCHEN

Guy had taken some time to review his notes on the different KPIs that Leo mentioned. In his mind, he kept getting an idea about sports and being on the offensive as much as possible, which is one of the objectives that Leo made during their last conversation: **"We want to be on the offensive always, not on the defensive"**. The line kept playing on Guy's head, since he was an avid sports fan and a nerd when it came to statistics, he was replaying both thoughts in his head to get better clarity.

Guy made the link between basketball and football with ball turnovers, and how an extra ball possession would allow a team to have more chances to outscore the opponent. The same with baseball with on base percentage, the more you get people on base the better the chance to score. This looked to be what Leo learned from reading Moneyball. In sales, the more you control the interaction with the customer to help them, to better understand their business and their ordering patterns, you have a higher probability of getting an order. This was logical for Guy and provided a guideline for what Leo was implementing.

It was time to visit Leo and see the system in action, so Guy coordinated the visit for the following Wednesday on a phone conversation.

That Wednesday, when Guy showed up at the door, everyone was expecting him, and his name appeared on the screen in the lobby: "Welcome Guy Galeti."

Leo started the conversation as Guy came in: "Hi Guy, so good to welcome you here, it is quite an honor to see you're taking the time to better understand what we have done here."

"It's my pleasure Leo and I have to say that I appreciate your generosity and the fact that you are open for this great system to be shared". Responded Guy

Leo: "Only if I share it will I continue to be on my toes. If I have learned anything at my industry association, it is that today's best practices will be tomorrow's old practices. We need to keep improving and I cannot think of anybody better than you to help us make our system better."

Guy: "Glad you think that way, let's not say more and let me see the system in action."

Leo: "We asked that you showed up early in the morning Guy, so you can participate in our daily sales huddle, it only takes 20 minutes. Since it is the end of the month, we will show you our sales weekly meeting as well. Our goal is to control the activities; if we control the activities, the results will follow by themselves, that way we avoid all end of the month closing crisis."

Guy: "Right, like we agreed, you need to control the activities and the activities will lead to results or sales goals."

Leo: "Correct, we control the activities that control the results, we know that if all MoneyCall salespeople make 20 to 30 calls a day, with 10 quotes and 100% F1 and at least 50% F2 we will achieve the results that lead to Delivery Calls (DC) and referrals or testimonials from our clients."

Guy: "So basically this is a predictable sales model, isn't it?"

Leo: "Like most things in life it is not 100% predictable, yet the more we track the numbers, the more predictable it becomes. We have the highest sales per employee of any location in the company. We know that once a salesperson controls their communication with their 100 clients, we can either hire a new person or divide their 100 clients into 2 salespeople and we will be able to increase their sales. The key is to use the 80/20 rule before we make the change and to see the results of the 5 Key Questions for the percentage of business that they do with us. We want to first have 100% of all our customers in our database on the Moneycall system and then we can decide if we need to hire more people to handle the referrals we get from our calls.

Guy: "So, you basically do not do much prospecting, your new clients come from referrals only?"

Leo: "Like I mentioned before, we know we are in a different type of business and many distributors or similar businesses never realize this; a recurring sales business should depend more on current customers by increasing the share of those customers, because we understand and serve them better. When you do that PROACTIVELY, you are more in control, and you can decide which customers you want to serve and which you need to leave for the competition. We know we are not a good fit for everyone, yet for those customers that value some of the variables that we control well, we can help them PROACTIVELY, then those are the customers that fit well in our Moneycall system.

Prospecting is not out of the question, please remember we opened 9 months ago, so perhaps in the future we may want to do some of it. The reality is that our system helps to bring the customers that value what our current customers value. For a car company, a software company or most IT solutions companies, life insurance, real estate and many similar industries, prospecting is the name of the game because each customer does a transaction once in a long while, so they need a pipeline. Our reality is much different, and we must use a different system than supermarkets to attract and serve our customers, the machinegun approach of supermarkets is not right for our business, we are more targeted and our Proactive Moneycall system is our rifle. Does that make sense Guy?".

Guy: "It does, now what do you mean by supermarkets having a machinegun approach, I did not get that?"

Leo: "Supermarkets control products because they are reactive waiting for the customers to show up and buy and do not have a lot of information about their customers. For example: They have 15,000 to 60,000 SKUs and close to zero information about their thousands of clients, on the other hand, we have a smaller number of clients per location and more information on them, their business, the owner and their staff. We give them training in marketing, we try to help with their growth plans, and we spend a lot of time with them, so we should be more proactive in analyzing why they buy product A and did not buy product B that normally goes with product A. We achieve that with a simple question to get feedback and see how we can help. Is that clearer now?"

Guy: "Yes Leo, thanks! It is like the sports analogy that I thought about before we made the appointment, we want to be on offense as much as we can to outscore our opponents."

They both smiled and together fist bumped.

Leo: "Well Guy, here you are, let's get into the conference room so you can see how we do our 20-minute sales meeting."

They both headed into the room and Leo stepped into his sales manager role and asked each salesperson how many calls, quotes, follow ups and orders they got yesterday vs the goal to see if everyone was on track. He immediately wrote all the numbers on the board and they all could see who was on top and who made more calls, follow ups, quotes, and sales.

Leo explained out loud to Guy that he selected at random a salesperson each day to call one of the customers that the salesperson logged in the CRM to see how the customer felt treated, and to see if what was logged on the CRM, was the same that Leo got from the customer. This prevented any salesperson from trying to show "fake" numbers on the morning meetings. The main reason is that Proactive calling requires more updated information on the CRM in order to make an informed "next call" to the same customer.

Leo then proceeded to show that 2 salespeople needed to step up to make the goal, yet by the trend they had, his face did not show much optimism.

As they walked outside the room, Guy asked: "Leo, you did not look very happy with the last 2 people on the list".

Leo: "You noticed?".

Looking a bit surprised, yet he continued: "They have been at the bottom for 3 months and even some new salespeople have done better than them. I am going to see if we can move them to other positions, yet I can see that they do not do the number of activities required to make the type of sales that the others who are at the top of the KPIs rankings. This is a very predictive system, so the people that do not perform the proactive activities that I mentioned, will not make as much money and on the same token, produce the sales for the company or the service to our customers that each salesperson needs to make.

Guy: "Well on the positive side, 2 is less than 30% of your salespeople and that is the normal amount any organization must substitute to remain competitive. That alone seems better than most to me."

Leo: "I understand, however you want them all to succeed, but in the end, I learned that not everybody wants to do the work that gets the big bucks, many just want to stay in their comfort zone. It is my job, as a sales Manager, to find the salespeople who want to be the best and help our clients more. In return, this will reward them. I am happy with the system, it encourages the average salesperson to grow, or if not, you will stand out quickly. **Quality people produce quality results and quality people with a great system produce outstanding results**."

Guy: "Well said, now you sound like Yoda."

They both laughed and Guy continued: "Would you let me see how they handle calls and keep the KPIs you review every day?"

Leo: "Sure Guy, let's observe Jose who has been here for 6 months and is among the top 3 every month.

Guy was able to see Jose's notes on the 5KQ from every customer and how he pointed out certain things they valued in each quote. It was impressive to see that most of the talking was done by his customers, and Jose just asked questions depending on what square (S1 or S2) he needed to make the call.

Jose suddenly got up from his chair and showed Leo a new video testimonial that a customer had just texted him on WhatsApp. Leo smiled and told Jose what a wonderful job he had done and to post it on social media.

Guy stood there listening to different calls and as he was about to leave, Jose turned around and said: "Please come with me, one of my customers is at the Will Call desk picking up an order for some parts and wanted to say hi to me."

Both Leo and Guy followed, and they saw how Jose greeted his customer with a high-five. The client told him how happy he was that everything was handled promptly again. As he had done previously, he wanted to take a moment to say hi and thank Jose personally for the outstanding service he was receiving. Jose took a selfie with his client and sent him a personalized text saying how much he always enjoys working for him.

Guy: "Well Leo, I certainly understand everything much better, and I think I can help many clients in electrical distribution, hardware sales and manufacturing with this system. I will start small like you did and ramp them up as they see success. Nonetheless, I kept some of the numbers you mentioned in the back of my mind and it seems you have won the challenge with your father as many of your numbers are the best in the company. So, when are we going to celebrate your new promotion?"

Leo: "Relax Guy"

He said smiling and continued: "It's only been 9 months and the challenge was for a year; we must keep the pedal to the metal and make sure we come out on top. I am optimistic yet I am like Andy Grove, the former CEO from Intel, who wrote the book "Only the Paranoid Survive". So, no celebrations yet, as we still have room for improvement."

They both laughed.

Guy: "I know you are not going to lose; I certainly get your point! I will keep you updated with my progress. Please, let me know when we can celebrate your victory, I am sure your father will proudly join us with joy, plus the company will also benefit from it tremendously. Talk to you soon".

They both said goodbye, went their separate ways and continued with their daily chores.

CHAPTER 12

CELEBRATION AND UPDATES X 2

Leo and his father Tony met a few days after the 12-month challenge was over and due to be measured. It was a very easy and pleasant meeting. Tony was full of joy, and he knew Leo had the numbers all along so there was no need for suspense. The key here was to answer the most important question: What to do next?

Tony: "I am so proud of you Leo for what you have done. It is truly remarkable! I am glad I took the risk and allowed you to do your own thing with your location, our number 18. Obviously, I am not ready to retire or to step down (he said that with a very serious look in his eyes directly at Leo). However, I know that this success calls for a change and I want to ask you, what should the next step be?"

Leo: "I thank you Dad for your support and openness with my ideas. I could never have done it without you and the experience you have from running the company for so long after your own father. I also thank you for allowing me to make my own path."

Tony: "Great, but again, what do you think we should do now?" He was forceful in his tone now.

Leo: "I should be the Sales VP of the company and upgrade all our locations to the Moneycall system."

Tony: "I like that idea, now are you planning on doing all other 17 at the same time?" There was admiration and doubt in his voice this time.

Leo: "No. To think that way would be unrealistic. We do need to change them quickly because we have a competitive advantage, and I am sure others will try to copy us. We still need to move fast, and to keep improving the system all the time so nobody can catch up to us."

Tony: "So, what is the plan to make everything work?"

Leo: "I think we need to change 3 locations at the time. It may take 6 to 9 months to produce the change and I have 2 other people that I think could help me with the transformation."

Tony: "Ok, who are they?"

Leo: "Laura who was the first person I trained in the system. Together, we learned all the different steps required for implementation. She also helped me make the right adjustments. The other one is Guy, he would never be our employee, yet we can hire him as a consultant. He has been doing similar work with his own clients and I think he could also help us to convert another location."

Tony: "That sounds like a plan, do they know about this idea?"

Leo: "Well, I needed to run it by you first to see if you agreed. If you do, then I would like to have a celebration. I want to throw a kickoff party, using the new system transformation as a company story and something for the remaining employees to look forward implementing in their locations."

Tony: "I have not stopped you so far and will not start stopping you now. So, you tell me, and I will approve it. This time, I can say that you have earned it and I would be proud to have this system implemented by you. Show me your plan and let's make it official to everyone, how does that sound?"

Leo: "Thanks Dad! I am so happy to hear that."

They both hugged and gave each other a few hard slaps on their backs. Not only did they feel pride, joy, and passion for the family business but also for the team they had both put together.

Leo immediately called Laura to inform her of her new role. She accepted on the spot with jubilation, even if it meant moving out of town for those new responsibilities to take care of 6 stores and transforming one at a time.

Now the tricky part was how to bring Guy into the team as a consultant. Leo called him for a meeting with the excuse that he was looking to see how he was implementing everything with his clients. As they met, they got right into the conversation.

Leo: "So good to see you, Guy! Like I told you, I want to hear the juicy details of how things are rolling with you in the implementation efforts with your clients' companies."

Guy: "Good to see you as well Leo, I am like you in many aspects, but I am more structured in certain things. I needed to understand better how the sales process worked for my clients. Like you guys here in LATAM Supply, my recurring sales clients' companies had three or four sale channels: the counter at the store, the inside sales/phone sales, the outside sales/personal visit sales, and the internet. Some did not have a counter salesperson as they only sold equipment and many only sold on the phone, yet the key similarity was that they were all 100% reactive."

Leo: "Interesting breakdown, that is nothing you did not know or expect." He remarked in a sarcastic way.

Guy:" I know, but to explain it better to others, you need to make things easier and break them down well. The key was that my clients all understood where I was coming from when I said REACTIVE vs PROACTIVE. The problem was that their sales teams were selling more than ever, and their profits were incredible, thus they were afraid to rock the boat too much."

Leo: "I can see a bit of my father in the hesitation your clients showed because *the biggest enemy of your future success is your current success*. Then, what did you do?"

Guy: "I showed them data on the number of customers who purchased very little with the 80/20 analysis. I explained the risk was just the salary of one salesperson to start. Plus, I would train this new salesperson and track the results until he/she achieves sales of $100,000 or more per month. I also added that it would take 3 to 6 months to get that number. With this explanation, they decided to jump in and allow me to start a Moneycall program for them."

Leo: "Beautiful, love the way you presented that! How did it go?"

Guy: "Just like we talked about and saw with your people, sales started to pile in, and the new salespeople were delighted with the system and with the tangible numerical results. Management was also looking forward to scaling up the new department."

Leo: "Great job Guy! What are you doing now?"

Guy: "I am going to propose a promotion for the first salesperson who I trained. She is going to take over as Manager of the department. She can do the job that I was doing. I was careful to always point out in our coaching meetings that this could be her job in the future and that she needed to do what I was doing with her. **All good salespeople are first their own sales managers**: they must show they can manage themselves first before they think about managing others."

Leo: "So true! That sounds like one more of those Yoda lines. Good salespeople must be great managers of themselves."

Guy: "I am glad you liked that. I repeated the same process of promoting from within with all my clients. I am pleased with the results. Now let's talk about you, what is going on here my friend?"

Leo: "Well, that is precisely the second reason I wanted to talk to you about. I am being promoted to Sales VP and will take on the transformation of all other 17 locations. I am promoting Laura, my first Moneycall salesperson, to Regional Manager of 6 locations. I also want to see if I could hire your services to help me transform the other region with 6 more locations. I don't know if you are interested, yet it would mean a lot to me and it would be very helpful since you understand the system perfectly."

Guy: "I think it's perfect timing Leo! I am finishing up the implementation with most of my other clients and promoting their people to take over my job. So, I can definitely help you. When are you thinking to get things started?"

Leo: "Perfect Guy! We want to start at around the beginning of the year. I will let you know when we have our kickoff celebration meeting with the whole company. With this plan we can start off the year on the right foot and get the whole company onboard with the idea."

Guy: "Like I said, perfect timing, I will wait for your call Leo."

They smiled, hugged, and said bye for now. It was a double celebration of success and promotions for the creators of the Moneycall system.

CHAPTER 13

THE BIG ANNOUNCEMENT FOR THE NEW LATAM SUPPLY

The party was about to start, and everybody was ready for the speeches, the already-suspected announcements, and the champagne toast. The music had been playing for a while now, but Tony and Leo always liked to start on time and as it hit 7pm, the lights at the podium illuminated the microphone and a big silence inundated the room. This was one of the biggest events in Boca Raton Florida yet only Tony's footsteps going up the podium could be heard. This was the moment everyone was waiting for.

Tony: "Ladies and gentlemen, fellow employees and manufacturing partners, our dear customers, all friends of LATAM Supply, thanks for coming. As you have seen the numbers of our last year our company is in very solid footing and growing above the industry average in most of the KPIs we share in the report with our industry association. Especially our new location led by Leo, has grown above all the metrics that we keep with great customer satisfaction and engagement, producing more testimonials than any other branch by more than 20 to 1 ratio. We want to announce to all of you that Leo will be taking on a new responsibility as Sales VP for the whole company. He will be appointing 2 more people to help him transform the company into the new proactive model that his branch has been so successful in implementing during the last year. Leo, I don't want to steal your thunder, so please let all our dear guests know what the immediate plans for LATAM Supply are."

A great round of applause shook the wine glasses on the tables. Leo approached the podium with Laura and Guy by his side as he stood in the middle to speak.

Leo: "Thank you Tony and thanks to all our distinguished guests for the generous applause. I am humbled by the fact that just over 370 days ago, I was taking a new role full of uncertainty, just inspired by an idea and the strength of some data regarding how to serve customers proactively. After many trials and errors, and decisions based on good analysis, we have polished a system that will always remain a work in progress. Laura and Guy have both been very instrumental in creating the process that led to the system we all created. The customers at our branch have a higher level of satisfaction than any other in the company, and our surveys indicate that our store employees enjoy their work more than in any other location as well. Those key indicators show, that we have a responsibility to take this system and implement it in the whole company."

Leo was interrupted by an even larger and more euphoric applause. He waited for 30 seconds, waved his hands down to be able to continue. This produced a complete silence, as everybody wanted to hear every word to follow.

Leo continued: "We also need to move fast as I am sure that our competitors will not stay idle and will copy what we are doing. That is why we have to, not just implement our Moneycall system, but also improve it so the competition can never catch up to us."

Another round of applause followed. Leo waited 15 seconds this time and went on.

Leo: "That is why I am appointing Laura as my Sales Director in the east region locations, and we will also be working with an outside consultant. Many of you have seen him around here before; he has the experience of implementing the Moneycall system in similar businesses, Guy Galeti."

He pointed towards his left where Guy was located.

Leo continued: "Guy will work with the southwest locations, and I will take the remaining southeast locations. We need the collaboration of all our employees to be able to make this happen. This means that we welcome any idea that you think we could use to make this system even more proactive to serve our customers. Please, come forward and let us see how we can implement it. Now I ask, what company that you know, does that for real?"

More applause stopped Leo for 10 seconds.

He quickly added. "We mean it, and the proof is location #18 here in Boca Raton, so let's get it done! We are counting on you!"

Everyone stood up to applaud as if it was a presidential victory speech.

The party went on and they all knew they needed to enjoy the moment before the Big Ben chimes got them back to reality on Monday.

CHAPTER 14

CAN YOU DO ANYTHING WITHOUT TECHNOLOGY THESE DAYS?

On Monday after the big announcement Leo, Laura and Guy got together to brainstorm the way forward. Guy wanted to bring some interesting topics to the table, so the two others listened to his views first.

"Guys, as you know we need to find ways to make the transition as fast and smooth as possible to all locations. I noticed that one of the keys to the system is record keeping. Some of it was done by the current phone system that you guys have programmed here, so that is a great advantage. Yet the CRM needs to be adjusted in order to make it easier to keep a good log of the different call types and what was the main issue in the call. I noticed that some salespeople complained about the time it took for all of this. I just heard from one of my clients that they are using Google docs, but that still generates too many pieces of information. I created an Excel log sheet, to show Victor the IT manager to see if he can program something similar into the CRM." Said Guy

"Interesting idea Guy", continued Leo. "I got some of the same responses from our people, although I did not pay as much attention as you did. Do you mind sharing the Excel sheet with us to see if we can start using it and as we begin to understand it, we could see what Victor can do with it, he usually is a magician."

Everybody laughed.

Guy: "Absolutely, let me show it to you and we can talk about it."

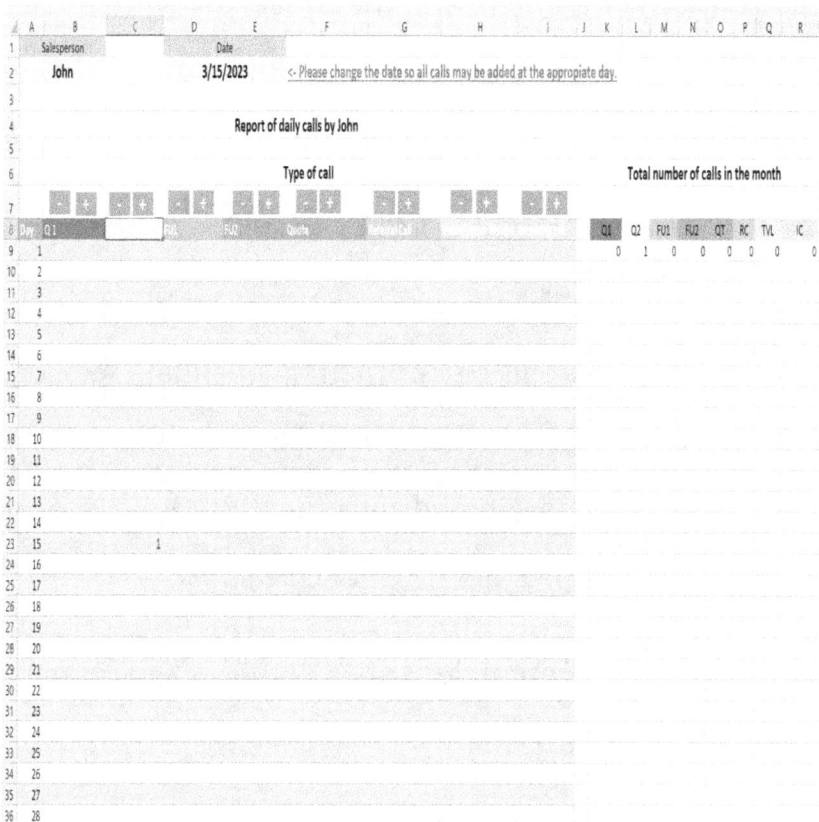

Guy: "This is a very simple log, it tracks the type of calls, now it does not say to who and the content. The main goal here is speed. You can just hit the +

sign to add a call to S1 if that was the call type. At the end, we have the incoming calls, and to the right is the summary for the supervisor who can see what everybody did every day. It keeps a summary until the end of the month, from there the supervisor keeps a copy and everybody else resets their sheet."

Laura: "I like this better than my manual Excel log, so we can start to use this while Victor finds a way to get it programmed into our CRM with similar ease of use plus details of each call."

Leo: "That is great, let's start with this and then we can move into whatever magic Victor can make."

Guy: " Here is the downloadable link: *https://4929193.fs1.hubspotusercontent-na1.net/hubfs/4929193/Moneycall%20report%20per%20salesperson.xlsm*
I don't want to rock the boat too much, yet it is

important to mention to Victor that perhaps we could use AI in the future to make faster decisions. For example, what parts have not been ordered for a while and which parts / equipment go together with current orders that the customer has never requested, so that S1/S2 calls may be easier to identify."

Leo: "Wow that is a great idea! It would reduce the training time it takes for salespeople to realize which parts to recommend in their S2 calls. We are sounding more and more like Star Wars here."

They all cracked up in laughter.

Leo: "The reality is that we need to be open to all these ideas if we want to continue to make things better and easier for the next phases. The phone system has been fully programmed to take calls directly to the assigned salespersons and tracks the individual calls to their customers. We even programmed text messages to be sent from our system. So, the plan will be: Roll out the Boca store phone system to every location, do our 80/20 breakdown, use the Excel log to start keeping track and let's train the new Moneycall salespeople in each of the designated locations we want to begin the implementation."

Guy: "You only want to hire new people for the new Moneycall positions?"

Leo: "We should keep an eye out for warehouse personnel who already know the parts and their uses. We also need people who do not mind calling and finding initial resistance until the clients understand the personal nature of our service, just like it has happened before."

Laura: "I am open to giving opportunities to current employees, however, we also need them to take an assessment test to see if they are a good fit for the position. I know the assessment is not 100% reliable but it is additional data for us to consider. If we do that for potential new salespeople, we should do it for the current employees as well."

Leo: "Agreed! let's roll out with what we have, we know there will always be a better way. What we have now works just fine, so let's get to it and let's keep Victor on his toes."

Guy: "We love to act, I like that! It feels like we are the Three Musketeers."

They all laughed and went on to start the implementation in all their branches.

After one year, 12 of the locations had been transformed and were using the model. The social media posts were done by location as the LinkedIn page of the company was inundated with all the testimonials that the branches generated. Sales were growing at a 27% clip in the 12 converted locations vs the remaining 5 that continued to use the reactive model. It took one and a half years for the Three Musketeers to get all branches up and running. The original Boca Location was the one further along the rest and it also benefited from the ideas that were continuously created in all other stores.

This is the story that has happened with many distributors, and it could happen to you, so where are your Musketeers to help your organization make the change? When will you hire your first Moneycall salesperson? What KP is will you use to start? Have you calculated your Maximum Sales Formula?

Our goal with this story was to inspire you with a new system that has helped many other companies achieve greater predictable sales results with a proactive system. Look for us on Linkedin and lets stay in touch.

INFLUENCERS

This is the session where I want to honor those who shaped my thinking and I want to provide a short summary with their main lessons to me, so perhaps you can decide to learn more about them.

- **Roy Chitwood**: I took his sales training as I started my Management Consulting sales career. He was the first person to show me a "sales process" and for an Engineer this made total sense. This got me more interested in consultative selling. Ask more and find out problems.

- **Andy Grove**: "Only the paranoid survive" was one of those management books that basically said, you need to reinvent yourself all the time. That is why we decided to end the book with ideas of how the system could still be improved. From there I always tell myself: The worst enemy of your future success is your current success.

- **Jeffrey Gitomer**: You can learn so much from Jeffrey. One of the most important things that I took from his webinars, podcasts and books is the fact that when you do not get the results you want, it is your fault, not the customers', your company's, or your products'. This idea drove me to look for ways to make sales easier and more predictable.

- **Art Sobczak:** The ex-football player that started a logical system to handle the phone. Art inspires me frequently with his podcasts and his book "Smart Calling", was invaluable for teaching me better ways to handle the phone as a salesperson. Sales training in other organizations, plus the daily activities helped me to polish my skills. Later, I found that combining a process with the quality of the call into a system, would improve my results drastically.

- **Joe Ellers:** I was fortunate to see a couple of presentations from Joe and nothing opened my mind more than the sales quadrant that I decided to include in the book. It is such a simple concept and it helped me concentrate on what salespeople needed to do to succeed. This later turned into the S1 and S2 calls with the simple questions that make sales so easy.

- **Neil Rackman:** Perhaps the most influential figure in selling to anyone who wants to be guided by data and not "guru talk". Neil and his book "Spin Selling", showed me the value of using statistics and data analysis to make sales decisions. I later followed everything he wrote and he did the Foreword of the book from the next guys I found.

- **Mike Schultz and John Doerr:** From the "Foreword "by Neil Rackman to their book, these authors pointed me to the Rain Group. A consulting firm that continuously does sales research, training and more. The basic idea is to use numbers and statistics to determine the best way to do a sales task. This was so logical to me; I was looking for correlation between seller's actions and sales. This was the reason behind tracking each of the types of calls and seeing what results we could expect from them.

- **Alex Goldfayn:** I could not believe it when I read Alex's writing about proactively calling customers. So, I studied all his books and did my best to have him in one of our talks at

HARDI. I felt that my idea had been validated. He has such an easy system that I don't understand why more people don't try it. The biggest lesson I got from Alex is the one included in the book. "Call when nothing is wrong just to say hello, I have been thinking of you." Obviously, you only do this if you mean it, and if you do your job well, you will care for your customers on a personal level. If you do not want to start a Moneycall sales department and system implementation, at least read his ideas and start there, it surely will help your sales.

- **Keenan:** "Gap Selling" was a transformative book for me. The idea that we need to identify "problems vs needs" was mind opening. He did not invent that concept although he made it clearer than anybody for me. I also found a lot of value in determining what is the cost implication of the problem. People pay to solve expensive problems. When I added the art of asking simple questions, just to understand the problems or what the customer valued, the Moneycall system took its final shape.

www.ingramcontent.com/pod-product-compliance
Lightning Source LLC
Chambersburg PA
CBHW072153290526
45794CB00004B/1496